K E I T

REALITY

THE JOURNEY FROM BONDAGE TO BLESSING

dustjacket

www.dustjacket.com

CONTENTS

INTRODUCTION

The book you hold in your hands is simply the work of a fellow traveler in this world. I have entitled this book *Reality*. The reality of the present circumstances of our world is very bleak. In such a world people search for hope in places that have no reality. For example, you and I have read books and have watched movies that depict a world that is beyond reality. We gain hope as we watch the superhero win the day despite impossible odds. Such moments often fill up with hope until we enter the real world, which has no make-believe.

The question I have for you is simple: Is there any hope in the reality of this world? Let's be honest—the real world is filled with failure, frustration, fatigue, and above all, false hope. However, if you are a Christ-follower, there is a certain hope in this world of reality. This hope has a real name: Jesus! Yes, there is a God in heaven who can lead you through this life with success even in the midst of failure, frustration, and fatigue. We find out about this God in His book, called the Bible. The Bible reveals to us a God who can handle any crises we face or ever will face.

Maybe you are in a moment where there is a real crisis before you. The crisis has you up late at night and has you so preoccupied that you have lost your joy in life. Be assured that you are not the only one. Maybe you are reading this Introduction because the future reality seems to be worse than your present reality. When you think about the future you become paralyzed in your present realty.

This was me in 2013 as I agreed to lead a mission team to the African country of Malawi for the first time. I did not sleep for days before the journey because I was so fearful of what was ahead. It was then I discovered an amazing truth about my God: Nothing is "in the future" to God. He is already there (see Psalm 139:7–14).

When God makes a promise to you in this journey, you can have confidence in God's fulfilling His promise. Yes, in spite of all that this real world throws at you, God is greater still. I recently met a mother who was our waitress at a local restaurant. When I asked how we could pray for her, she responded, "Yes, please pray for me—my son is graduating this weekend." I knew what she meant by her request. The future was fearful and frustrating because it was beyond her control. One of the toughest questions in this real world is this: "Will you trust God, or will you trust your instincts?"

The book you hold in your hands is simply a collection of the truths I have gained from my studies about a people group who made a journey from a place of bondage to a place of blessing. These people in reality had no possible hope of victory apart from God. Their journey was filled with two things: God's faithfulness and the people's flaws. In the midst of this real-world stuff we find our hope in a God who kept His word!

Who are these people? The people I am referring to are the children of Israel. Their journey takes place in the Bible book of Numbers (given its name because of two censuses God orders to be taken of His people). The time line covers the forty years they spent in the wilderness because they failed to walk by faith and the short journey afterward to the moment when the blessing would begin.

In this study you will see their flaws up close and personal. Please do not allow their flaws to discourage you. You will find such courage as you walk with Israel through her problems. You will see God's faithfulness in every place they journeyed.

Here is a life verse that describes the truth of this book: "And I am sure of this, that he who began a good work in you will bring it to completion at the day of Jesus Christ" (Philippians 1:6).

I want to challenge you at the beginning of our study to open your heart to God's leadership of your life. I want to encourage you to believe that God can take you from a real world of bondage to a real world of blessing. Finally, I want to cheer you on to keep the finish line before your eyes.

This book is in my usual format. Each week you will have the focal text from Numbers. Next you will have a devotion that overviews the focal text. Then you will have five days of readings from the Bible. Each day you will be challenged to answer two questions with the hope that you will share with others what you are discovering.

I want to thank my wife, Sherry Long Joseph, for walking this journey in the real world with me. I could not imagine having to walk the journey from bondage to blessing apart from her. She is my best friend, my cheerleader, my accountability, my lover in life, and most of all my partner in chasing Christ. Thank you for the journey.

To God alone be the glory!

Keith Joseph
May 24, 2018
John 3:30

STUDY 1

Preparing for the Journey
Focal Text: Numbers 1–4

As I arrived back home from a 5:30 a.m. Bible study, I knew we had only a few minutes before we were to leave for the eight-hour journey to Lynchburg, Virginia. I quickly packed my last-minute things, and we got into the car. Sherry was going to begin the journey behind the wheel so I could study. She started the car and then turned to me with this important question: "Which way should we go?" I responded, "I don't want to go through Atlanta." Sherry responded, "It adds almost forty minutes to our trip if we bypass Atlanta." For me this was not a sacrifice. I just did not want to go through urban congestion of I-75 in Atlanta.

As you and I begin this journey in the real world of the book of Numbers, I want to get this correct. It is so important for us to have the same road map (GPS) because we will end up in different places if we have different versions.

Here is my road map. The book of Numbers continues the story of God's people on their way from bondage to blessing. Yes, it is true: I am getting ahead of you already. Let me go back to the beginning point on the map for Israel.

Numbers 1:1 tells us of God's people, who are thirteen months into their journey. You remember their journey, do you not? It began back in Egypt. It was Moses who led the people out of bondage (Exodus 6–12).

Israel's bondage began when a new Pharaoh came to power who did not know the God of Joseph. Suddenly life became miserable for God's people. God saw their affliction and bondage (Exodus 3:8–9).

This is where the journey became so amazing: God was coming to deliver them. It is a picture of one who was greater, who was coming through the heavens for us (Hebrews 4:14–16). When the last plague was carried out by God, Egypt had to give the people up, or better said, give the people back to God.

This is such an amazing picture for us because it was Jesus who went to the cross so that we could be delivered from bondage (Romans 4:24; 8:32).

When God delivered Israel, she was given new life. A people who were not a people were now a people. It is the same with all who come to know Jesus as Lord and Savior (Galatians 2:20).

As we look at their road map, I want to give you a warning about this new life journey. The journey from bondage to

2

blessing is dangerous, because we have an enemy who wants to entangle us in the bondage of the wilderness of this real world. We do not have to fear either our enemy or the wilderness (Galatians 1:4), because Jesus is for us (Romans 8:31). But we must be aware of the wilderness (Ephesians 6:10–13).

Focus on the map! God now takes Israel on a journey that brings her to Mount Sinai (Exodus 19). God has carried her every step of the way (vv. 4–6). It will be here where Israel will spend the next year. During this time much will happen including many moments of failure, frustration, and fatigue. However, we see the faithfulness of Moses. It is here where the people enter into a covenant with God.

God promises to guide Israel to certain victory (Exodus 23:27). However, it all almost comes to a crashing end when the people grow weary while waiting for Moses to return from the mountain with God. Again I say, this is almost the end of the people before the start of the journey (Exodus 32). However, God makes atonement for their sin (v. 20). It is only by grace that the journey begins (Exodus 33:17). Exodus 40 ends with Moses writing about God's presence being with Israel as they begin the journey.

This is our map. This is how we get here to Numbers 1:1. It is time for Israel to make the short journey from Sinai to the Promised Land.

As they get ready to go, God orders a census of all the men who are twenty years old and above. It is these men who will lead the battle to take the promised land. From these first four chapters we discover two decisions one must make if he or she is going to walk the journey from bondage to blessing:

1. One must be accounted as one who will sign up for the journey (Numbers 1:1–46).

The men had to step up and sign up as those who would engage in the journey. In this real world we have a choice. Either we war with Jesus leading us, or we walk in the wilderness of a mess sometimes without Jesus.

Here is an inside scoop for you: God never says we are to be perfect nor does He ask us to war in our power. All God asks us to do is to walk by faith in this journey. "We walk by faith, not by sight" (2 Corinthians 5:7 ESV).

These men would end up making the wrong choices on the journey. God had provided for the only way for Israel to survive in the wilderness, but they had chosen a different path. What was intended to be only a few weeks' journey would turn into a forty-year journey.

Pay attention as you prepare for your journey. Life goes by so quickly (James 4:13–18). The earlier you sign up with Jesus the better. The wilderness will take more out of you than you want to give. The wilderness claimed 603,548 of the 603,550 who signed up for the journey.

2. One must embrace his or her assignment on the journey (Numbers 1:47–4:49).

In these chapters we see God's specific assignments for different groups of people. God always has specific assignments for His people. We see God's assignments for the leaders in chapter 1. We see God's assignments for the priests and Levites in chapters 2–4.

Question: What assignment has God given to you? The assignment is to be carried out according to His plan and His power. D. L. Moody wrote the following:

> Nothing that is done for God is small. . . .
> Anything that God is in isn't small. If we go to work right at home, we will have success. There isn't a child of God who can't do something if he will. (Dwight L. Moody, *The Homework of Dwight L. Moody* [Albany, Oreg.: Books for the Ages, 1996], 70)

This week you will be challenged by reading about the assignments God gave the people in Moses's day. In this real world you had better be committed to your assignment in the war, because Satan wants you in the wilderness.

DAILY READING GUIDE

DAY 1
Read Exodus 1 and answer the following questions:

- Describe in your own words how devasting it must have been for the Israelites to have their freedom taken from them.

- Describe how hard it is to serve God in a godless place.

DAY 2
Read Exodus 2 and answer the following questions:

- Why did Moses's parents willfully disobey the law given by the Pharaoh?

- Would there ever be a time when you would disobey the law? Give examples and offer scripture in your answer.

DAY 3
Read Exodus 3 and answer the following questions:

- What must have been going through Moses's mind when he had an encounter with God?

- What would God have to do in order to deliver His people? In your answer describe what God did in delivering you.

DAY 4

Read Exodus 4 and answer the following questions:

- Why was Moses so reluctant to believe God could use Him?

- Aaron goes with Moses to Egypt. Do we need Aarons in our lives? Give reasons for your answers.

DAY 5

Read Exodus 5 and answer the following questions:

- What is our usual disposition when we have done God's will and life gets harder?

- If you were in Moses's place in Exodus 5, what would you have done? Give reasons for your answer.

STUDY 2

Potholes in the Road
Focal Text: Numbers 5

My early years of life were spent in the mountains of eastern Kentucky. Life there was a journey. One of the constant problems (back in the day) was with the local road systems. Travel was often hindered by the numerous potholes in the road.

As I visit Malawi, Africa, twice per year I am reminded of my early days, because we travel on the same type of roads there. Here is what I have discovered about potholes:

1. Potholes make your journey much more difficult.

2. Potholes can eventually break your vehicle.

3. Potholes can cause you to give up on the journey.

4. Potholes can keep you from reaching your destination.

Spiritually speaking, we each have our own potholes (called sins) to deal with along the journey of life. It was this way in Moses's day. The people had made the correct preparations for the journey. They had signed up to follow God's directions, and they were accepting their individual assignments for the journey.

Here is where we need to heed a warning: "Watch out for the potholes."

Iain Duguid writes about this moment in Israel's journey:

> Even though the people were following or-
> ders, it did not mean order would naturally exist
> in the camp. There would be times of disorder
> and sin. Therefore, the people needed to be in-
> structed about disorder and sin. We are no dif-
> ferent than they were. Although we would like to
> be able to talk about happy things all the time,
> the reality is that we too are sinners who need to
> know how to deal with that fact. (Iain Duguid,
> *Numbers: God's Presence in the Wilderness* [Whea-
> ton, Ill.: Crossway Publishing, 2006], 66)

In Numbers 5 we find the answers we need in dealing with sin (spiritual potholes) along the journey from bondage to blessing. This chapter reveals three truths for the journey:

Sin separates us from God along the journey (vv. 1–4).

The chapter begins with a hard-hitting command from God: "Put out of the camp . . ." The NASB translates this as follows: "Send away from the camp . . ."

These words cause a sadness to fill my heart. Could it be possible that the road could get so filled with potholes that God would say, "Send him or her away"? Once while I was in Africa the road became so difficult that we had to send most of our team back with the bus. As I drove forward in another vehicle with three others, I thought, "John is going back." My heart was sad in knowing what he and the team would miss out on.

Much deeper than this is the reality of what sin does to us. The Bible identifies this as eternal separation from God.

God said, "Send away anyone who is defiled because he or she could defile the camp." The word *defiled* is not a word we are familiar with. When a person is defiled in biblical terms, he or she has stepped into a pothole that makes him or her unacceptable to God. A modern word would be *corrupt*.

It was not that these people were worse than others. It was that they had a type of disease that could spread to the rest of the camp. Brothers and sisters, sin always costs everyone in the camp of the body of Christ. Sin is bigger than a mistake. Sin is all-out war against God.

Sin must be dealt with along the journey (vv. 5–10).

I imagine seeing the people leaving the camp in brokenness (v. 4). It must have been so hard for their families and friends. As I image them leaving, I find myself asking, "What about the rest of the people in the camp? Were they without sin?" Verses 5–10 give us our answer:

"When a man or woman commits any of the sins . . ."

Did that sentence move you to tears? I realize we are all going to commit sin along the journey. The King James Version calls these sins "trespasses." The Hebrew word carries the meaning of an act of unfaithfulness and treachery before God." God says, "When you feel the weight of your trespass, you need to confess your sin and make restitution for your sin."

The people were to give back what they had taken from others. They were even to give back more than they had taken. This would ease the hurt with their fellow travelers, but what about their treachery before God?

Each person was to go before the priest in order for the priest to sacrifice a ram called "the ram of atonement." This sacrifice would cover the sin. But what about the next time?

Suddenly I realize a great problem along the journey. The people would get through one pothole, and they would get into more potholes along the way. So what hope did they have in order to rise above the potholes? The answer is in the third truth for our journey.

Sin can be correctly dealt with only by Jesus along the journey (vv. 11–29).

Moses points us to one particular extremely deep and large pothole. We all know about this pothole. It is called adultery. What makes the hole even larger is our inability to know if adultery had been committed in this situation. According to Roy Gane, there are no fewer than five problems with this situation:

1. It deals with suspicion rather than clear-cut guilt.

2. Guilt or innocence can be impossible for a human tribunal.

3. The stakes are high—adultery was a capital offense.

4. Unresolved suspicion can wreck a marriage.

5. Suspicion could be lethal to the woman.

(Roy Gane, *The NIV Application Commentary: Leviticus, Numbers* [Grand Rapids: Zondervan, 2004], 521)

Here is what we must come to: God alone is qualified to judge matters of the heart. The potholes are too deep, too deceptive, and too damaging to others. This is why Jesus came to drink the bitter cup of sin for us (Mark 14:34–36). Jesus has correctly dealt with our sin.

This day I know I have the capability of falling into many spiritual potholes if I walk in the flesh. But if I walk in God's Spirit, I will walk in paths of righteousness for His namesake. I pray this week has you walking in His paths.

DAILY READING GUIDE

DAY 1
Read Exodus 6 and answer the following questions:

- Why did Moses need the reassurance of God?

- Why did Moses say to God, "I am of uncircumcised lips"?

DAY 2
Read Exodus 7 and answer the following questions:

- Why does God allow us to go through times of proving our faith while on the journey? Consider Moses's having to prove his faith to Pharaoh as part of your answer.

- What experiences in your journey can you point to that testify of God being with you?

DAY 3
Read Exodus 8 and answer the following questions:

- How would the potholes called "plagues" move you to let go of God's people if you were in charge?

- Why was Pharaoh continuing to harden his heart against God's plan?

DAY 4
Read Exodus 9 and answer the following questions:

- What distinctions does God make between the journey of the non-believer versus the believer in Christ?

- What distinctions has Christ made in your life? Give a few examples.

DAY 5
Read Exodus 10 and answer the following questions:

- Why do Christ-followers often become the targets of people who are really mad at God? Consider verse 7 in your answer.

- Was Pharaoh's confession before God in verses 16–18 genuine? Explain.

STUDY 3

Promises, Promises
Focal Text: Numbers 6

In the real world it can be so easy to get trapped into doing things you really do not want to do. For example, have you ever attended a meeting and ended up being elected as chairman of the committee? I went to a housing owners' association meeting one evening to ask one question and before the evening was over, I was elected president of the group.

In the real world it can be so easy to get trapped into making promises that you had no intention of making, even worse–keeping. In the early 1980s there was a secular song written titled "Promises, Promises" that expresses skepticism about promises made.

In the real world it is very hard to know if someone means the promises he or she makes or if they are just empty brush-offs. In our studies we are discovering how God always keeps

His promises. But at the same time, we will soon discover how Israel often made promises they never intended to keep. This is the real world of disfunction.

God's intention for His people was clear. He had delivered them from bondage, and He was leading them to earthly blessing. The journey was intended to be filled with sweet fellowship. If this fellowship were to last, the people had to deal with the potholes (Study 2) in the journey. But they would also need to understand the seriousness of their commitments to God.

Today our journey mirrors that of Israel. Christians are on a journey from bondage to blessing, and it begins at the cross. (If you have not yet begun your journey with Jesus, please see the Appendix at the end of this book, which reveals how to begin this journey with Him.)

The sweet fellowship that God intends to fill this journey with (1 John 1:3–4) takes place as we walk with Him in holiness (1 Peter 1:13–16). Now this is very important— along the journey the Lord intends for us to walk closer and closer to Him.

In Israel's day there was a special expression used to identify this truth: "the vow of a Nazirite." The Hebrew term "Nazirite" means "a separated one."

The people of Israel were offered the opportunity for a selected period to walk closer to God. It is important to note it was totally up to the Israelite to make his or her own choice about it. It is also important to note that this separation was only for the set time chosen by the individual.

Jacob was the first of God's chosen people to make a vow (Genesis 28:20–22). There were those like Jephthah who made vows they later regretted (Judges 11). It was Hannah who made a vow to God when she asked for a child (1 Samuel 1:11). There were also those like Absalom who made lying vows (2 Samuel 15:8).

Vows are very serious to God. He did not require His people to make vows, but when they did, God took them so seriously that He gave guidelines for vows in Numbers 6. Jesus condemned the abuse of vows in Mark 7:10–13.

In Numbers 6 God gave three guidelines for one who made a vow:

1. A person was to stay away from all alcoholic beverages or anything that related to its production, such as grapes and vinegar.

2. A person was to not cut his or her hair.

3. A person was to have no contact with any dead person or thing.

If a person broke any of these guidelines, he or she was to offer a sacrifice for his or her sin, shave the head, and then begin the period of the vow again. Guidelines one and three reminded the person of his or her need of being separated from the things of the world. Guideline number two was a testimony before others of his or her vow before God.

At this point the question needs to be asked: "Why would a person make such a vow?" Roy Gane gives us insight: "The vow could simply be an expression of devotion and gratitude to the Lord, or it could be tied to a request for some kind of tangible or spiritual benefit from God" (Gane, 533).

"Often Nazirite vows were conditional: if God does (such and such), I will become a Nazirite for (x) period of time. Although Nazarite vows continued to be made into the Christian era, neither Christians nor modern Jews make them today" (Joe M. Sprinkle, *Leviticus and Numbers: Teach the Text Commentary Series* [Grand Rapids: Baker Books, 2015], 42).

For me personally the question is "What can I as a Christ-follower take from Numbers 6? I believe there no fewer than four applications to this chapter:

1. Salvation can never be earned by any vow of works (Ephesians 2:8–9).

It is God who through Christ works a glorious exchange in us. He came to take my sin debt (2 Corinthians 5:21) and to break the chains of my sin (John 8:36). He has made me new in Him (Titus 3:5). He took my sin so that I might take His righteousness. In this I am made ready for the journey with God.

2. Salvation places us on a new journey in which we want to walk closely with God (Romans 6:19–22).

This walk is called "the walk of sanctification." We do not make vows for salvation, but we do make a vow to follow Jesus (Matthew 16:24–27). We are called to strive to walk with God (Hebrews 12:14). Our vows are simple. We will do whatever He directs us to do (2 Timothy 2:15). What is so awesome about this is His empowerment through the Holy Spirit to live this life (Galatians 5:16).

3. Christians sometimes along the journey lose sight of their commitments (vows).

Ecclesiastes 5:1–7 encourages us always to keep our vows. It is through our commitment to God that the world sees what it means to be a Christ-follower.

4. Christians have something to look forward to at the end of the world.

Jesus made a vow to the church through two angels in Acts 1:11. He will someday return to keep His vow. Each day I walk with Him knowing there will come a day when He will say, "Come up here to live with me."

I hope you take time this week to consider your vows before God. I pray you keep your commitments, and I pray you will be challenged always to make commitments that honor God.

ASSIGNMENTS FOR THE WEEK

DAY 1

Read Exodus 11 and answer the following questions:

- If you had been an Egyptian living in that day and you knew what was coming, would you have made a vow to God? Give reasons.

- Would any vow have kept the last plague from coming? Give reasons.

DAY 2

Read Exodus 12 and answer the following questions:

- Why was it so important for Israel to obey God's commands for the Passover?

- Why did Israel not keep the Passover (12:14) during the days of Numbers?

DAY 3

Read Exodus 13 and answer the following questions:

- Why was it important for the firstborn to be consecrated to God? What does this mean for our day?

- What was the importance of the Feast of Unleavened Bread?

DAY 4

Read Exodus 14 and answer the following questions:

- Why did Pharaoh change his mind about his vow to let God's people go?

- Why were the Israelites so fearful in this chapter? Were they afraid God would break His vow to them? Explain.

DAY 5

Read Exodus 15 and answer the following questions:

- If you could write a song to Jesus, what would you write?

- Why did the people so quickly forget the blessings of God? Explain.

S T U D Y 4

The Blessing
Focal Text: Numbers 6:22–27

There he stood in all of his glory. The congregation was longing for this man to speak the blessing over them. As he did so, some people were lifting their hands to heaven and some were shouting, "We receive the blessing!" In my mind I was trying to find where in Scripture this blessing was taught.

In the real world there are multitudes of different religions and even different variations of beliefs within a given religion. We who know Christ have come to know that Jesus is the way, the truth, and the life (John 14:6). We have also come to know that we must follow only what the Word of God directs us to follow. Israel would find herself many years later facing bondage because she disregarded the Word of God over and over. Isaiah 43:24 says, "You have burdened me with your sins; you have wearied me with your iniquities." But for now the people were attempting to obey God.

In these beginning days Israel would encounter many false religions with their dead gods. If Israel was to be successful on her journey from bondage to blessing, she would need to see through false worship and know how to get beyond the pull of darkness. How could the Israelites do this? The answer is simple: They needed God's blessing.

In the same manner, Christians today face a real world filled with false religions and the pull of darkness. Brothers and sisters, we are in desperate need of God's blessing. The question of our hour is this: does this blessing come through the lips of men or does it come some other way?

Numbers 6 teaches us of the blessing coming from God Himself. The Bible says God spoke to Moses and instructed him to direct Aaron and the Levitical priesthood to pray to Him for a threefold blessing for the nation of Israel. God clearly states the blessings He will give to Israel on the road if they are willing to obey Him.

Notice with me the components of the threefold prayer:

1. Ask Me (Yahweh) to protect and oversee your life.

The words *Keep me* speak of literally being a bodyguard. The Bible teaches of God's power to protect His people (Revelation 3:10) and His wisdom to direct His people (Psalm 119:105). Joe M. Sprinkle comments, "When God blesses people, He does not merely pronounce goodness on them; rather being God, He is able to bestow the good that

He wishes. Thus, when God blesses us, we actually get the goods" (Sprinkle, 217).

God wants to bless His people, and He will bless them if they are walking as He has called them to walk. However, God never keeps someone who does not want to be kept.

2. Ask me (Yahweh) to show favor in being merciful and gracious in your life.

God promises to be gracious (v. 25) by showing His favor (His face) toward you in being merciful. God's graciousness comes to those who seek forgiveness (Matthew 6:12). Roy Gane writes,

> God is gracious in showing His favor as He shows compassion toward sinners (Ps. 41:4). David prayed asking God for mercy in Psalm 51:1. If God would not show mercy, David's transgression would not be taken away. (Gane, 541)

The opposite is also true: if God turns His face away from a person, that person will face His judgment (2 Thessalonians 1:9). This is important to note, that God's favor can be lost if the person is disobedient to God. We see this in Deuteronomy 28. It is to God we are accountable. He is the one we vertically pray to. He is the subject in this threefold blessing, and it is He alone who gets the glory.

3. Ask me (Yahweh) to graciously give you a well-rounded life filled with peace.

When the Lord looks upon His people, He looks with the same eye that He looked upon Adam with as He created him and breathed the breath of life into Him. He looks upon His people with the same countenance He had when He created the Garden of Eden and placed Adam and Eve in it. God wants our lives to be filled with peace—a well-rounded peace that begins with God (Romans 5:1) and finds its expression in a peaceful life with others (Romans 12:12–21).

This blessing comes to those who walk in the way God has called them to walk.

Brothers and sisters, God wants to walk with us in this same way. This happens as we live in a way God can bless. The teaching of Jesus in Matthew 5:3–11 concerning the Beatitudes shows us how to obediently live in a way in which God will bless.

Now it's time to answer my question from the beginning of our devotion. Where in Scripture does it teach that a person can pray a prayer of blessing on a group of people? The answer is Numbers 6:22–27. However, the blessing being asked for is conditional between the person we are praying for and the God we are praying to.

It would be this way in Numbers 14 when Israel did not obey God. God said, "I will no longer go with you." Israel said, "We will go, and we want Your blessing, Lord." But God would not bless them (vv. 41–42). Moses could have prayed, and every pastor who has ever lived could have prayed that day for those people, but God would not bless.

Brothers and sisters, the blessing is there. The question is "Will you obey the God of heaven who wants to bless you?" In this week's reading assignments you will be challenged to understand why Israel was at times blessed and at other times not blessed.

ASSIGNMENTS FOR THE WEEK

DAY 1

Read Exodus 16 and answer the following questions:

- Why did God choose to bless a grumbling people? Does God ever bless you in spite of your grumbling?

- Why did some of the people refuse to keep God's commandments and laws?

DAY 2

Read Exodus 17 and answer the following questions:

- As Moses cried out to the Lord for the people, so does Jesus cry out for His people. How is Jesus crying out for you today?

- Why did the Lord choose to fight for Israel, and why does He choose to fight for you?

DAY 3

Read Exodus 18 and answer the following questions:

- Why do we need Jethros in our lives to ensure the continued blessing of God?

- Moses was in a position of great leadership. How did God's blessings turn into a trial for Moses, and how do these same blessings turn into trials for us?

DAY 4

Read Exodus 19 and answer the following questions:

- What does it mean when God says, "I bore you on eagle's wings"? How does this relate to your life?

- Why did God give specific instructions concerning approaching the mountain?

DAY 5

Read Exodus 20 and answer the following questions:

- How many of the commandments must we keep to earn the blessings of God?

- Why were the people so afraid of God speaking to them? Are you ever afraid to speak to God? Explain.

STUDY 5

A Great Plan for Summer Success
Focal Text: Numbers 7–9

As I write this chapter I am sitting at my home office desk with both books and bags packed in anticipation of another week of summer camp. The truth is—my books and bags have been here since I got home two days ago, because I knew I would be going right back out today. The real world is always busy, but even more so in the summer months.

Question: How successful are we in the summer months?

Your answer and my answer depend on what our goals are for the summer. I can speak only for myself. It is my goal to love God and to make disciples of all people this summer and every summer.

However, the truth is that I sometimes get so caught up in the moments of summer that I forget my mission for the summer. This is life in the real world. The real-world summer is filled with sweat, sacrifice, and shear exhaustion as the days seem to run together. I remember an episode of the ABC sitcom *The Middle* in which the family wastes the entire summer trying to have fun. I always laugh at the episode until I realize—this is so many of us.

How would you respond if I said, "God has a foolproof plan for a successful summer"? This is exactly what I am saying as we come to Numbers 7. God has always had a great plan for summer success for those who love Him and are committed to His eternal plan.

We see this plan clearly in our devotion text for the week. Keep in mind that God's people are at Mount Sinai. This is the desert. They have been here for almost one year. God has told Moses to direct the people on a march from the place of bondage to the place of blessing. Before they go, God directs them in what they need for the journey. By chapter 7 most things are in place. However, there are five more areas of their lives that needed attention before they are ready for the march through the desert.

Here are these five areas: Offerings for the opening of the tabernacle, the setting-up of the lamps, the preparations of the Levites, the celebration of the Passover, and the glory cloud of the Lord.

Each of these areas could be dealt with individually, but for our devotion we place them together because they form for us a threefold plan for summer success. Here is the plan:

**God wanted the people always to
gather in His house along the journey.**

The tabernacle has been set up as we come to chapter
7. This reminds us of our studies from Exodus 40:17. The
nation is celebrating its one-year anniversary of deliverance
from bondage. When the tabernacle was set up, God's glory
filled it (v. 34). It was now time to make the first offerings in
this amazing place.

In this place they would come often to gather with God
along the journey. In a previous study entitled "The Journey
to Becoming" we discovered four encouragements when we
gather in God's house:

- God's glory reminds us of the unfathomable
  greatness of His person. This is where our
  contentment comes along the journey.

- God's glory awakens a hunger for the unfathomable
  greatness of His person (Philippians 3:8–13)—
  "that I may know Him" (v. 10).

- God's glory calms the fears of the uncertain world
  around us (Philippians 4:6–7).

- God's glory directs our passion to the certain
  future we have with Him (Philippians 4:13).

During the summer months the average church sees
its lowest attendance and its least support—at a time when

it needs it the most. The church is God's chosen place for us to gather. It is His place where His servants are to be cleansed for their service to God. It is in this place that we gather to remember what Christ (our great Passover lamb) has done for us. It is in this place that we are called back to a focus of purpose. Please make gathering a priority in your summer plans.

God was growing His people as they gathered with Him along the journey.

If God's people were not gathering, there could be no growing in the Lord. They were called to make offerings, to make sacrifices for their sins, and to follow the light given to them. It is the same in our lives today as we are called to give of our time, talent, and treasure to God (Romans 12:3–11).

As we walk in His light, we have fellowship with Him and with others. God positioned the lamps for the lighting of the way for the people in the tabernacle and in the way they should move forward. We see this over and over in Scripture, for example Psalm 119:105; Job 29:2–3; John 8:11–12. Oh, how I pray you make daily time to gather and to grow in your walk with Christ!

God was going with His people as they walked in obedience to His plan for the journey.

The glory cloud of God was His "Shekinah" presence with them. Our God desires to direct our summer days and our summer nights. He desires to protect us and to empower us for true summer success. But we have to be willing to gather and grow so that we can go. I can testify of sensing the presence of God in our summer days and nights. The people whose lives have been changed, the feeling of personal success, and the refreshing power of God to our souls are proof positive of the success of God's plan.

This was, and still is, an amazing plan. It has always been and always will be God's plan, not only for the summer months but for every other month in every year of our lives. I want to meet with God each week in the summer. I want to grow in my walk with God so that He will go with me guiding me to success in every moment on the calendar.

I truly pray this devotion has given you a plan that you will grab onto as you walk through this real-world summer. Take time to reflect on this plan as you walk through each day's reading plan.

ASSIGNMENTS FOR THE WEEK

DAY 1

Read Exodus 21 and answer the following questions:

- What was God's viewpoint concerning slavery?

- What does the New Testament teach concerning slavery?

DAY 2

Read Exodus 22 and answer the following questions:

- What does the Scripture teach concerning the desire to get even?

- How does the world's viewpoint of social justice differ from the Bible's viewpoint? Give illustrations.

DAY 3

Read Exodus 23 and answer the following questions:

- Does God still require a "Sabbath rest"? Explain and defend your answer.

- Did God keep His promise to Israel, and does God keep His promises today?

DAY 4

Read Exodus 24 and answer the following questions:

- How must have Moses and the elders felt when God called them to the mountain?

- In your opinion what must have happened with Moses during those forty days?

DAY 5

Read Exodus 25 and answer the following questions:

- If you had been alive in the time of Exodus 25, what would you have offered for the tabernacle?

- What was the purpose of the ark of the covenant?

STUDY 6

Listening for the Trumpet to Sound
Focal Text: Numbers 10

When I was a child I had the honor of being raised in a small country church. Each Sunday there was a certain time before the morning service when one of the deacons would walk to a certain place in the back of the church that had a rope hanging down from the ceiling. On the other end of the rope was our church bell in the bell tower of the building. Each week the chosen deacon would pull the rope, and the bell would ring signifying to our community that it was time to gather for worship.

Question: What is it in your life that leads you to pay attention to God? What system do you have in place that always calls you to attention as you travel this road we call life?

Maybe you ask, "Why is this important?" You and I need constant direction on the road. We need God to protect us from Satan's traps, which lie just around the corner. We need God's intervention when we are about to get in the flesh. In these moments we must have something in our lives that calls us to attention to God.

For the nation of Israel there was the cloud of glory, which guided their way. We remember from last's weeks devotion how that when the cloud moved from the tabernacle, the people would move from the tabernacle. One would think they had everything in place to move. For the last eleven days they had been following God's final preparations. Everything seemed in place until God said to Moses, "There is one more thing I want you to do" (See Numbers 10:1–2).

Why did they need to make two silver trumpets? This is a fair question. The people had God's glory cloud to direct them. Honestly, this was my initial thought until God revealed the following: What if some of the people were in their tents sleeping when God moved in the cloud? What if they were not looking to the cloud in the midst of their busy day? Suddenly I realized that this was very important to the future of God's people.

It is the same in our day. When I was a kid, church bells were used to call us to attention. Times have changed. We seldom hear church bells today. Today it is God's people, including pastors and evangelists, who have the clarion call of God on their lives to sound the trumpet to come to attention because God is speaking. "Pastors and preachers trumpet

God's Word in preaching, and they pray on behalf of God's people who fight for God" (Sprinkle, 244).

Focus with me on those two trumpets. The silver trumpets were going to be used for no fewer than three reasons:

- To summon the people for a meeting. When one trumpet sounded, the leaders would assemble for a meeting. When two trumpets sounded together, all the congregation would assemble before the tabernacle.

- To summon the people to break camp. In succession the camp would break and move when the trumpet blast came for their sections to go.

- To summon the people to war.

I imagine seeing the priests picking up the trumpets to blow. I imagine the people being anxious to respond quickly to the trumpet sounds. The priests alone were to blow the trumpets. They were to be on the job. On this day the camp was assembling, and they were going to begin their march to the promised land. I cannot imagine the scene as all this nation in an orderly way were marching in the desert.

There must have been great excitement as they were responding to the trumpet call. These people were being called to walk with the God who was taking over! Approximately forty years from this day a new generation of God's people would be summoned to battle. These people would stand before the massive city of Jericho (Joshua 6). Seven trumpets would blow, and the walls would fall down. These trumpets have much to say for our lives as well.

Brothers and sisters, we are called to march in this real world, waiting for and listening for the trumpet to sound. Question: Are we ready for the trumpet to sound? On the night of Passover, Exodus 12, God's people were ready, and on this day they were ready as well.

The apostle Paul challenges us to put on the full armor of God, having our feet ready with the gospel of peace (Ephesians 6:15). Be honest—do you have everything ready? The trumpet could sound as I write this devotion or while you are reading this devotion.

One more question: Are the people in our world ready? Jesus teaches us in an insightful parable to make sure we are ready (Matthew 24:36–51).

Moses pauses and looks at his father-in-law when the trumpets sounds. He asks him to do one thing: "Come with us." This is such an amazing invitation generated by the trumpet call. Brothers and sisters, pay close attention here: heaven is not just for those who are already ready. There is still more room (Luke 14:22).

This is so true for us: without a healthy awareness of the coming trumpet sound, we will never share our faith. Here is what I have found in the New Testament that is so important for us to consider:

1. We need to be ready for the Lord's return
   (1 Thessalonians 4:17–18).

2. We could receive the call at any moment
   (1 Thessalonians 5:1–6).

3. We are waiting for the "apocalyptic trumpets to sound, which sounds the death knell of oppression against God's people" (Gane, 574). See Revelation 9–11.

When the Lord returns, the Bible says, we are "waiting for and hastening the coming of the day of God, because of which the heavens will be set on fire and dissolved, and the heavenly bodies will melt as they burn!" (2 Peter 3:12). Brothers and sisters, for the sake of others pay close attention to God's trumpet calls.

Until the Lord returns, the Bible says, "according to His promise we are waiting for new heavens and a new earth in which righteousness dwells" (2 Peter 3:13). Oh, my brothers and sisters, I am encouraged to listen even more closely as the day approaches!

Our readings this week will challenge us to listen for the trumpet call.

ASSIGNMENTS FOR THE WEEK

DAY 1

Read Joel 1 and answer the following questions:

- Why was God judging the people, His people? Be specific.

- Do we see any signs of judgment in our world today? Give examples.

DAY 2

Read Joel 2 and answer the following questions:

- In both chapters 1 and 2 the prophet refers to "the day of the Lord." What does this mean for their day and our day?

- How does a person or a nation "return to the Lord"?

DAY 3

Read Joel 3 and answer the following questions:

- What day is the prophet referring to in verses 1–4?

- How does verse 14 lead you to live your life in reflection of what you have learned in this week's studies?

DAY 4
Read Habakkuk 1–2 and answer the following questions:

- What struggles did the prophet have in chapter 1, and how can you identify with him?

- Why was the prophet willing to wait for God's answer in chapter 2? Are you presently willing to wait for God's answer?

DAY 5
Read Habakkuk 3 and answer the following questions:

- Why does the prophet celebrate the Lord's coming and why should we celebrate the Lord's coming?

- With the dark days of tribulation still to come, how does 3:17–19 give us great encouragement? Be specific in your answer.

STUDY 7

When the Flesh Gets in the Way
Focal Text: Numbers 11

I can still remember the moment in time. I remember where we were and who we were doing ministry with. I can still remember the two guys who were having a conversation. I, along with several other young pastors, was standing there listening to two of our heroes in the ministry. Suddenly one of the men began sharing things that were extremely inappropriate. The other man looked at him and said, "Brother, you have gotten in the flesh."

Question: Does the flesh ever get in the way of your journey from bondage to blessing? I can answer only for my life. The answer is yes. On that particular day I lost much respect for this one person, and within a few months this man was out of the particular ministry he was in. It has been years since I thought about that man, but one thing I have often thought about is this: the flesh can really get in the way of our journey in the real world.

As we come to our study for this week, we see Israel in a moment when she gets in the flesh as a people. This is her first journey from Mount Sinai. It is a three-day journey. The people were following the cloud. What an honor it must have been for these people to have been chosen to enter the promised land! Four hundred thirty years earlier, God had promised Abraham a time when his lineage would own their own land (Genesis 12:7). Now it was about to happen. Israel has been made into a mighty army. As we read this chapter, suddenly the atmosphere changes.

The Bible says, "The people complained." It is clear that they were complaining about three things:

- Poor accommodations
- Poor food
- Poor leadership

The scene that followed seems so out of character for God and for Israel. These very people who had been experiencing the overwhelming mercy of God found themselves facing the wrath of God. What had happened? Roy Gane comments,

> Here our Lord comes down hard on the grumbling (in the flesh) of the Israelites. When they first complained about bitter water, God did not punish them but simply met their needs by making the water sweet (Exo-

dus 15:23–25). When they complained about not having food, He gave them manna (Exodus 16). God was giving them a learning curve. But now it was time for them to deal with what was now happening. They are exhibiting a rebellious behavior in refusing to trust God. (Gane, 587)

In summary—Israel has gotten in the flesh!

When a person gets in the flesh, there is often the blame game that comes into play. It was Adam who in Genesis 3 blamed Eve for his sin and she in turn blamed Satan. Yes, it is true that there were specific people in the camp who led the people to sin. Moses identified these people as "the rabble." The King James Version identifies them as "the mixt multitude." These were the people who were walking on the outskirts of the camp stirring up the people. The fallout of getting in the flesh was extremely costly to those who died under the wrath of God. (See also Hebrews 10:29–31.)

As the story unfolds before us, we see no fewer than four results of getting in the flesh:

1. Your life will be characterized by a complaining spirit.

"When a man's folly brings his way to ruin, his heart rages against the Lord" (Provers 19:3). The people complained against the Lord's direction and His provision of food. Their complaining spirit became too much for Moses, who went to the Lord with his own complaints (Numbers 11:11–15).

2. You will be chastened by the Lord.

The people came to this moment only three days into their journey. The International Standard Version identifies these people as "riff-raff." This people began, probably on the first day out, to have a "craving." This word speaks of a strong desire that was consuming them (Psalm 78:30). In this moment their minds were altered. They looked back to where they had been as if it were a wonderful place. God was about to turn them back around.

3. You will crave things that will choke out your faith.

God has been providing for their needs all along the journey. Now they suddenly cry out, "What you offer is not enough!" They make the following observation about their lives: "We have no energy. Without meat we are done for."

Question: Which do we crave more, the spiritual food from God or the physical food given by God (Psalm 1:3)? If you had been there in the moment, you would have heard all the crying in the tents of Israel. I wonder—would you have said, "You people are in the flesh"?

Their spiritual sight was gone in that moment. They were asking for what they thought they needed. But very soon they wished they had not asked for meat.

4. At some point you will regret your craving for the flesh.

The Lord speaks: "What you want will soon be coming out your nostrils." We would say, "It will be coming out your ears." Moses is shocked. He cannot imagine how God could accomplish such a feat. If one did the math, he or she would discover a conservative number of more than 105 million birds to feed these people.

Imagine the scene as a people in the flesh see the hand of God at work. This was a miracle. But while the food was in their mouths the Lord struck the people with a plague. We are not sure what God inflicted the people with. One thing is for sure: it was deadly. Notice the name they gave this place: Kibroth Hattaavah—literally "the graves of craving."

The people truly regretted their decision of getting in the flesh. Brothers and sisters, as I contemplate this chapter I am reminded of Psalm 78:1–7, which echoes what we need to take away from this chapter. The God who is good to us along the road reminds us to stay out of the flesh. When we get in the flesh, God chastens us because He loves us (Hebrews 12:5–11).

I pray you will examine this week's reading plan with an eye to walking in the Spirit (Galatians 5:16).

ASSIGNMENTS FOR THE WEEK

DAY 1

Read 2 Timothy 1 and answer the following questions:

- Why was Timothy so discouraged? Is it easy to get in the flesh when you are discouraged? Explain.

- How does the pull of the flesh effectively lead people like Phygelus and Hermogenes to turn away from the Lord?

DAY 2

Read 2 Timothy 2 and answer the following questions:

- What are the civilian pursuits Paul refers to in this chapter? Give illustrations.

- What are the youthful passions Timothy must avoid? Do these passions still affect us in middle age and beyond? Explain.

DAY 3

Read 2 Timothy 3 and answer the following questions:

- Is it possible for a Christian to become corrupt in mind and to be disqualified regarding the faith? Give reasons.

- How does the Scripture help us overcome the flesh?

DAY 4

Read 2 Timothy 4 and answer the following questions:

- What role does the flesh play in people's desire to hear what they want to hear from teachers?

- Paul writes, "The Lord stood by me." How does this encourage us in our Christian lives?

DAY 5

Read Psalm 78 and answer the following questions:

- Even after Israel saw the miracles of God, she still doubted God. Why was this the case?

- How are we able to learn from Israel's mistakes? Focus in on verses 1–7 in your answer.

S T U D Y 8

Lies, Slander, and Racism
Focal Text: Numbers 12

A mother consoling her seven-year-old son who had for the first time experienced the evil of racism said, "Son, we live in a very cruel world."

This mother was very accurate in her description of the world system. Each day children everywhere face life in a very cruel world. Without a doubt each person who reads this chapter has illustrations of encounters with a cruel world. There is one that stands out to me, even after many years.

It was my first trip to Romania. I had been there for almost two weeks with our mission partners, and it was the last day before returning home. One of the pastors was showing me around the city. Suddenly I realized we were now in a rough part of town. I can still see the two men who were lying on the street corner with only cardboard boxes to sleep on. The pastor I was with just walked on by. I stopped him and asked,

"Who are these men?" I'll never forget his response: "Oh, they're only . . ."

This pastor was refusing to share Jesus with people based upon a racist view that clouded the gospel's call to all people. This is the reality of a very cruel world. Every day ours is a world filled with lies, slander, and racism. It's the same type of world the children of Israel lived in.

As we travel back to their day and their story, we're reminded of it. Israel is on the journey from bondage (Egypt) to blessing (the promised land). The trip is filled with real-world moments. This week is no exception.

The chapter begins in what seems to be the middle of something: "Miriam and Aaron spoke against Moses."

Question: What was your first thought when you read those words? Did you feel the weight of the sin, or did you simply wonder what they were saying against Moses? Your answer reveals where you are on the road of life.

There are two roads here. One is the road being taken by those slandering, and the other is the road being taken by those who show forth the meekness of God.

Miriam and Aaron are on the slandering road. We are not positive of the why of their slander. It seems that they are upset because Moses is married to a woman who is not of their heritage. If this is the core reason, we see racism at work. But if it is because Moses is dividing the leadership responsibilities (11:16–23), then slander is at work. The road they are on gets worse, because they accuse Moses of taking leadership all to himself. Without a doubt this is a clear lie.

Oh, how it hurts when you are the victim of racism, slander, and lies!

The natural response would be to speak out in defense of your character and to lash out against those who are lashing out at you. But wait—you know this is not the road you are to take. God has a different road for you. We see it before us as Moses turns on this road.

It is the road called meekness. The Hebrew word for meek can be translated as "gentle, mild, and modest." It is used to speak of someone who is under control. Yes, there were moments in Moses's life when he failed to be meek, but the norm of his life was meekness.

In meekness Moses stands behind his Lord. Notice how the Lord protects those on the road of meekness. Notice how Moses is vindicated on the road of meekness.

We see the Lord's protection.

The Lord speaks about Moses's life in verse 3. The Lord calls out Aaron and Miriam. There was clearly something wrong in their hearts (Mark 7:22). Their position got them in trouble with God while Moses's position led him to His continued favor (Psalm 25:8–9).

The Lord reminded both Aaron and Miriam of how He spoke differently to Moses. To them God had spoken in visions, but to Moses it was face to face. God's work in Moses's life had transformed him into a meek man. If you struggle with a life of pride and selfishness, the Lord can transform you if you come to Him (Matthew 5:5).

We see the Lord's vindication.

The Lord said, "You should have been afraid. This is my leader, and you should not have spoken against him." Notice what happened next: Miriam became leprous.

In this moment the Lord took strong measures to teach the people the evil of a life of slander, racism, and lies. For an entire week "all Israel had plenty of opportunity to reflect on the deadly leprosy of rebellion against God's leadership through Moses" (Gane, 592).

Immediately Aaron recognized that he and his sister had taken the wrong road. Repentance came quickly, but the question remained: what would Moses do?

Notice this meek man as he cries out to the Lord in verse 13: "O God, please heal her—please." This is the road I want to daily take in this very cruel world. Moses did not allow their wrongs to rob him of his meek heart. Moses loved his sister and brother. In this moment the Lord honored Moses's prayer.

Now we come rushing back to our day. We also live in the real world. You and I face what Moses faced on a daily basis.

Be assured that God allows us to intersect those on the road of slander, racism, and lies for the single purpose of showing the world the different road they need to be on.

In Romans 12:14–21 Paul instructs us on how to live on that road. In Hebrews 3:6 we discover the one greater than Moses who transforms us and places us on the right road. His name is Jesus.

This week you will interact with Scripture, which will lead you to overcome the devil, who wants to cripple you. You will soar above those who would embitter you. Finally your voice will become stronger in a world that cannot silence you.

ASSIGNMENTS FOR THE WEEK

DAY 1

Read Daniel 1 and answer the following questions:

- Why was Daniel so adamant about not eating meat?

- Why did only four Hebrew slaves stand up for their faith? Explain.

DAY 2

Read Daniel 2 and answer the following questions:

- Would it have been hard for you to help those who hated you if you had been in Daniel's shoes? Explain.

- Why did God choose to work through Daniel to reveal the future?

DAY 3

Read Daniel 3 and answer the following questions:

- How hard is it to stay committed to Jesus when your bosses seem to have the upper hand?

- Name a time when God met you in the fires of life and delivered you. Write down your experience.

DAY 4

Read Daniel 4 and answer the following questions:

- Why did the king think he was invincible?

- How does God humble people today?
  Give examples.

DAY 5

Read Daniel 5–6 and answer the following questions:

- What must have been in Daniel's heart as he shared
  the interpretation of the dream with the king?

- How would you have responded if you had been
  in Daniel's shoes in chapter 6?

STUDY 9

Courage: Part 1
Focal Text: Numbers 13

On this road called life we face many moments when we do not know what is coming next. In those moments we need something deep within us to help us face those times. It was the same way for Israel.

The Lord was directing Israel on their journey from bondage to blessing. When the presence of God (in the cloud) moved, they moved. In Numbers 13 the cloud had settled along the border of the promised land. What would be next for God's people?

You and I do not have to debate the answer. Chapter 13 begins with these words: "The Lord spoke." The words that followed must have been met with different responses. Here is what God said: "Send men to spy out the land of Canaan" (v. 2).

I wonder who said, "I want to go!" I also wonder who snuck to the back of the crowd. Was it a rush of courage that swept over the crowd or was it a rush of fear?

Without a doubt you and I have experience with both responses. In the real world we face many events labeled "unknown." In these events we make a choice either to meet the event with faith or to meet it with fear. In faith people move forward. In fear people are paralyzed.

If you have ever felt the weight of fear, know that I can identify with you. Since my earliest childhood memories I have always struggled with courage. Many have been the moments when I was filled with paralyzing anxiety in the seconds leading up to a confrontation. But one thing has always won the day for me.

This one thing has over and over kept me from giving up. This one thing has been there for twenty-six years of ministry and has been there for countless mission trips. I have leaned on this one thing in good times and bad. This one thing has been there in every life issue.

What is this one thing? It is *the courage of the Lord.*

The Bible says, "If God is for us, who can be against us?" (Romans 8:31). In my life I have always found His courage to be more than enough for me.

God's courage always comes to those who have confidence in Him. God's confidence comes with His promise: "The land of Canaan . . . I am giving to the people of Israel" (v. 2). Be assured that God's promise is also for you and me as well.

In this moment the Lord chose twelve men (leaders of each tribe of Israel) to be courageous. Their job required courage. These men were to go on a covert operation to accomplish the following: They were to assess the strength of the people, the position of the people, the places of strongholds, and the ability of the land to feed a conquering army.

Certainly God's commands to you and me will be radically different from His commands to those twelve spies, but yet we still need courage in the day-to-day commands of God in the real world. Hear God's words of encouragement to us through Moses: "Be of good courage" (v. 20).

In this moment I feel the need to hit the pause button and remind you of the following reasons we need this encouragement:

1. Every day we face a world system filled with obstacles.

2. Every day the Father sends us into the world for His glory.

3. Every day we face an enemy who seeks to wipe us out.

The nation of Israel found themselves in the world system, having been sent there by the Father. Before them was an enemy who wanted to wipe them out. For forty days the nation waited for the return of the spies. Would they return alive, and if they did make it out alive, what would their report contain?

Suddenly someone shouts out, "I think I see them coming!" I can hear the crowd: "Are all twelve coming?" The other one responds, "Yes—God has been faithful again!"

Please allow me to hit the pause button one more time. There is a fourth reason we need encouragement:

4. Every day other people are counting on us to be successful in the field of battle.

The nation's future was hanging in the balance with these twelve men. Would the people be encouraged to go forward or would they be encouraged to turn back?

You know the story. If not, read on ahead in chapter 13 (vv. 27–33).

In this moment I must ask you—Will you place your trust in God's love and care for you? If so, courage will rise up because you know this truth: "If God is for us, who can be against us?" Take time today to strengthen yourself in the Lord.

Next week we will focus on the differences between the things that rob us of courage and those that release courage.

This week take the time to think about all the effects of giving into fear and those of being courageous. Finally consider your own life. Are you happy with where you are or are you not?

ASSIGNMENTS FOR THE WEEK

DAY 1

Read Daniel 7 and answer the following questions:

- Why did God choose Daniel as His prophet and why does God choose people to represent Him today?

- Explain who the Ancient of Days is and why we can have courage in Him.

DAY 2

Read Daniel 8 and answer the following questions:

- How does God's knowledge of the future give you courage in this day?

- Why was Daniel overcome with sadness (v. 27) when he understood the vision?

DAY 3

Read Daniel 9 and answer the following questions:

- Why was Daniel such a man of prayer?

- How does prayer give assurance to the Christian?

DAY 4
Read Daniel 10 and answer the following questions:

- What value does fasting have in the courage of a Christian?

- Why did the angel tell Daniel to fear not in verse 12? What does fear do to courage?

DAY 5
Read Daniel 12 and answer the following questions:

- What is the time of trouble spoken of by Daniel in verse 1?

- What will happen to the church in the end of days?

STUDY 10

Courage: Part 2
Focal Text: Numbers 13–14

Everything was set, all the plans were perfectly laid out. It was a 100-percent-guaranteed plan. Failure was impossible. All that was left was simply executing the plan. However—the plan was not carried out.

What was this plan, and why was it not carried out? It was for God's people to claim their inheritance in the promised land. Why was it not carried out? There were ten courage-robbers who captured the courage of an entire nation. What followed was a forty-year detour into the wilderness of judgment.

Brothers and sisters, some plans have an expiration date. For example, the offer of salvation has an expiration date. Hebrews 9:27 states, "It is appointed for man to die once." Once death comes, there is no more opportunity to receive God's plan (see Appendix 1) for your salvation. God has plans for your life, and they have expiration dates. The question is always—"How much time do I have?"

Be courageous, and you will certainly have plenty of time to carry out God's plan in your life. The road you are on is being timed. Pay close attention to what you read today, because it can fuel your courage.

The children of Israel have come to the edge of the promised land. Everything is set. God is for them, and He is leading the charge (Deuteronomy 31:6–7). The time of the year was harvest season, which means God had provided all the food they would need for the campaign. The spies had gone in to make the plan. All that remained was for the people to walk in God's courage.

However, it was not to be—because of the spoiled report given by the courage-robbers.

Dear brothers and sisters, you have a choice in your journey in life: either you allow the courage-robbers to rule the day or you choose to follow the path that releases God's courage in your life. Keep in mind that the clock is ticking. Which path will you choose?

This week we will focus on seven traits of courage-robbers, and next week we will focus on six traits of courage-releasers.

When the spies return we quickly come to understand that ten spies were courage-robbers and only two were courage-releasers. Look closely as the nation gathers around these men as they deliver "the word" about their journey.

I was amazed at how Moses spoke God's word. This speaks of God's communication with people. There was great weight in what they said. The courage-robbers had seven traits:

1. They viewed life from a "however" perspective.

Even though the land was filled with milk and honey, and even though God had promised victory, there was still the "however." Such people always see the possible roadblocks instead of the open road ahead. The possible obstacles always outweigh the opportunities. Despite Caleb's wisdom, these men believed the people were not able. This is what happens when we look to ourselves alone. We forget that God is able (Genesis 18:14).

2. They viewed life from the point of their own inabilities.

Such inabilities come often from a life filled with spoiled moments in the journeys of life. These men brought an "evil report." They were breaking God's plan in pieces. They truly had grasshopper faith. What they needed was giant faith (1 Samuel 17:45–47).

3. They viewed life from the point of failure always being someone else's fault.

The people blamed Moses for getting them in this place where they could not possibly win (by their own understanding). The people turned on God and complained of God's goodness as being only in the past.

4. They viewed life from hearts filled with complaints.

The people cried out all night long. This happens when courage has been removed from your life. Such people have lost, or have never had, a true viewpoint of the goodness of God in stretching them into a place of trust. In such moments God wants us to look up (Isaiah 40:22).

5. They viewed life from a place of gloom and doom.

In their minds they wondered why God had brought them there. They thought they must be under a curse. Gloom-and-doom people are dangerous to be around. We see this as the people think of stoning Moses. You and I must guard ourselves from those who would take our courage from us.

6. They viewed life from a place that crushes what could have been.

The people had despised God over and over again. They were chronic unbelievers. The inheritance they had been offered was now off the table. I cannot believe it as I read 14:25. Everyone twenty years old and older would die in the wilderness of judgment.

Be careful, my friend, with those you walk with. The courage-robbers will take your children's futures and will lead you to finish your life as a failure.

7. They viewed life from a place of always moving too slowly.

The people wanted to obey after it was too late. They said, "We will obey." But it was far too late. Many people spend their lives saying, "Maybe someday." But "someday" never comes.

Brothers and sisters, is this the group you want to hang out with? Is this the group you often lead?

This week's readings take us into another group where the people challenge us to have courage in God's plan. Feast on their way of thinking.

———————◆———————

ASSIGNMENTS FOR THE WEEK

DAY 1

Read Philippians 1 and answer the following questions:

- What attribute of God does Paul encourage the people with in 1:6? Define it.

- How does standing firm in the gospel work hand in hand with God's courage?

DAY 2

Read Philippians 2 and answer the following questions:

- What type of courage did Jesus have to have in coming to this earth? Explain.

- How is courage needed in "working out your own salvation"?

DAY 3

Read Philippians 3 and answer the following questions:

- How did courage play a part in Paul's decision to renounce Judaism and embrace Christianity?

- How does knowing Christ lead to greater courage? Explain.

DAY 4

Read Philippians 4 and answer the following questions:

- Describe the power of anxiety and its negative work in your life.

- How can Philippians 4:13 reshape your life? Explain.

DAY 5

Read Joshua 1 and answer the following questions:

- Joshua followed a courageous leader. Describe someone who is courageous for Jesus today.

- In what areas of your life do you need God's courage? Make a prayer list from your answers.

STUDY 11

Courage: Part 3
Focal Text: Numbers 13-14

"Who is this guy?" This was the question a friend asked about someone who was very different now than when he was in high school. Classmates were wondering if this was even the same guy. After a time of investigation, they discovered it was the same guy—but at the same time he was different now.

Along the journey of life some people change for the better and some people change for the worse. Question: How is it with you?

When we consider Israel as a nation, she is changing. When she came to the Desert of Paran (13:26), all appearances were of a mighty army ready to come into her blessing from God. But now, in one major rebellious moment, we see a people who are headed back out into the wilderness for forty more years.

What happened to this people? The answer is simply this: Israel followed the direction of the courage-robbers. Last week we met these ten men, and we examined the seven traits all courage-robbers have in common. We ended our devotion with a warning to stay away from such people.

This week I offer you great encouragement from the same chapters because this was not the only story in chapters 13–14. If you look closely you will notice the story of two men who were different. Their names are familiar to us: Joshua and Caleb. Both men were what I call "courage-releasers." If the Israelites had listened to them, the promised land would have come in their generation.

Walk with me as we focus on Caleb's story in hopes that all who read this will become courage-releasers for this generation and all who come after.

Roy Gane offers a helpful commentary to set the story of Caleb's life in motion: "Caleb was born a slave in Egypt, and his name meant 'dog.' But God set him and his people free. Most of the Israelites never got the hang of what freedom was all about, but Caleb did. He lives in the same environment as the others, but he views it with a different perspective" (Gane, 94).

We see Caleb in 13:30 quieting the people in order that he can share with them the truth of a life that releases courage. Notice six traits of a person who is a courage-releaser, as seen in Caleb:

1. Caleb had a high view of God.

Caleb wants to go in this moment. He says, "We are well able." He knew the power was not his but God's. He knew nothing was impossible with God.

2. Caleb had experience with God.

Caleb knew God, and he knew of God's work since his days as a slave in Egypt. With wide eyes of faith he had seen the ten plaques that broke the willpower of his captors. He had crossed the Red Sea with His people. He had stood at Mount Sinai when God spoke. God had brought his people to this point, and Caleb knew God would not let them down.

3. Caleb understood the will of God.

In chapter 14 Caleb tries a second time to turn the people away from the courage-robbers. If they could only by faith trust in the will of God, they would find courage being released into their lives.

If the Lord was pleased with Israel, she would be blessed to enter into the land promised by God Himself. Caleb knew this was the will of God.

4. Caleb was an obedient servant of the Lord.

When God speaks in 14:24, He calls Caleb, "my servant." He was following God. But the people were bent on rebelling against God (v. 9). They were doing the forbidden. This rebellion was provoking God (16:30). In this scene we see the leaning of the nation. They were in unbelief (Deuteronomy 9:23). They rejected the path God intended for them to walk. In this dramatic scene they chose to follow their own viewpoint, as would the generations that followed (Isaiah 65:2).

Courage-robbers always reveal a rebellious heart.

5. Caleb understood the power of God.

Caleb knew there was no reason to fear the enemy. God was on their side. Caleb knew the enemy would be bread in their hands, that God had removed His hand of protection from them. But in this moment Caleb's people did not want to be on God's side.

"Faith is courage that conquers. Disbelief is cowardice that correctly assesses the impossibility of a situation but fails to take God into account, thereby snatching defeat out of the jaws of victory" (Gane, 602).

If God was with them, the enemy was going down. But now God would not be with them because of a rebellious heart. All the adults would die over the next forty years. But two men would go through and enter the promised land with a new generation. One of those men was Caleb.

6. Caleb had a different spirit.

The Spirit of the Lord was directing his life. He was a man of faith who held firm to God. His future was sure. We see it in Joshua 14:7–8. Caleb, along with Joshua, would "live still" after judgment was completed. Caleb's spirit was different. So is the life of courage-releasers.

Many scholars believe Caleb would spend the next forty years pouring this spirit into the life of the generation that was coming. Oh, how I want to live this way, and I pray you will be willing to live this way as one who is a courage-releaser!

ASSIGNMENTS FOR THE WEEK

Day 1

Read Joshua 1 and answer the following questions:

- Why did God choose Joshua over Caleb to be the next leader of Israel? Give reasons for your answer.

- Why did this new generation follow Joshua's direction (vv. 17–18)? Explain.

Day 2

Read Joshua 2 and answer the following questions:

- Why was Joshua not afraid to send spies? It had not turned out well for Moses.

- What kind of faith did these spies exhibit, and in what areas do you need courageous faith this week?

Day 3

Read Joshua 3 and answer the following questions:

- Would you have had the same kind of faith as the priests in chapter 3? If so, what is keeping you from stepping into the water of faith?

- Does the Lord still perform miracles today? Give examples if you responded yes.

Day 4

Read Joshua 4 and answer the following questions:

- Why is it important to remember the past miracles of God?

- What does Generation Z know about our God?

Day 5

Read Joshua 5 and answer the following questions:

- Why did the enemies of God's people show such fear (vv. 2–3)? Does Satan fear God today?

- Why was it important for the people to be circumcised? What signs do we need in our lives concerning our faith?

S T U D Y 1 2

Scaling the Wall of Reality
Focal Text: Numbers 15:1–29

The writer of Proverbs gives us revelation for our day in 13:12. This is what he writes: "Hope deferred makes the heart sick." The Message translates this part of the verse as follows: "Unrelenting disappointment leaves you heartsick."

This must be an accurate description of Israel's people at the end of Numbers 14. The Bible says in verse 45 that the enemy "beat them down"(NIV). The truth is that the beat-down was of their own doing. Israel had zero courage. The wall of reality for them was bigger than their faith in God. One can almost feel the unrelenting disappointment as we visualize the people making their way back into the wilderness of failure.

Brothers and sisters, when people lose hope, the enemy always pounces on their minds and hearts. This morning my father shared with me the tragic news from his hometown of a man who took his own life because he had lost hope of ever being physically better in this world. I wondered what lies the devil had placed in that man's mind. I believe it is true: when one has no hope in his or her heart, the mind is open to being occupied by lies of all kinds.

This was Israel. Can you identify with the people as they carry their belongings back into the wilderness? Was there any hope of the future for these people, and honestly is there hope for people who find the wall of reality bigger than their faith?

While you are trying to work through your answer, open your Bible to Numbers 15 and read verses 1–2. Suddenly we see a spark from the ashes of failure lifting to the winds of hope. Roy Gane comments, "After divine condemnation of the adult generation pronounced in Chapter 14, Chapter 15 implicitly emphasizes God's grace in giving the younger Israelites hope for the future" (Gane, 619).

Brothers and sisters, if you have read this entire chapter, you might be tempted to ask, "What sense does this chapter make?" Here is the sense: the people of God were devastated. The devastation of rebellion will become worse in the narrative as the chapters continue. Future generations would need the hope given in this chapter in order for them and for us to continue scaling the wall of reality without losing hope.

This chapter brings hope to two groups.

1. This chapter brings hope to you and me personally.
God promises that the people will enter the land for one

reason: God will give the next generation the land. This land will be their home, which means there will be hope for future generations. Once in the land, the people will come before God with offerings of worship to Him. In verses 3–12 Moses describes the exact procedure of the offerings of worship to God.

In verse 14 we find even more hope as we are introduced to the second group. Moses identifies a member of this group with the title "alien" (NASB). This is not something from outer space. It's simply a designation for anyone who is not a Jew.

2. This chapter brings hope to all people.

Anyone who would embrace the God of Israel as his or her Lord would enter into this hope for the future. Brothers and sisters, what great news for our lives as fellow Gentiles! Paul wrote the wonder of this truth in Ephesians 2:13—"But now in Christ Jesus you who once were far off have been brought near by the blood of Christ."

For both of these groups there was a promise of the land providing all they needed, seen in verses 18–19. Both groups were to give God a portion of what He had given to them.

As I read these verses there is only one word that comes to my mind: "wow." Here before us is the record of a people who are miserable failures before God. To our surprise, they are being offered hope. If you want to increase your "wow" factor consider this: This people will for generations to come continue to fail God, but God will remain faithful to them. Let's take our "wow" factor to another level. You and I also fail the God who continues to remain faithful. There is only one word for me to describe this: "wow."

Brothers and sisters, we need this chapter. This chapter gives us insight into a big deal: "Theology can scale the wall of reality." This plays out before us in verses 22–29.

Two theological points bring hope to us in the midst of our failure:

1. When we fail, God provides a way of forgiveness.

When Israel failed as a people to obey God, they could be forgiven. When individuals failed God, they could be forgiven. We see this in the word *atonement*. This powerful word speaks of God's work through Christ in earning our salvation through the sacrifice of Himself as payment for our sins. Romans 3:25 tells us of Christ being the payment (atonement) for us. Jesus did this for the sins of people (Hebrews 2:9).

Gane amplifies this truth through his insightful commentary: "Today we remember Christ's sacrifice by partaking of what we know as the Lord's Supper. The bread and wine remind us of the hope of the atonement. By not eating a lamb, we acknowledge the Lamb has come (1 Cor. 5:7)" (Gane, 624). When we fail we must seek God's provision for our forgiveness.

In Israel's day the people were often making sacrifices to God because they had failed. Today we come before the throne of God in prayer seeking to receive God's atonement for our daily sins (1 John 1:7–9). We know Jesus's atonement was sufficient for our every sin (Hebrews 9:9–13).

This is so important as we scale the wall of our reality. Jesus is not in heaven preparing a place for perfect people. He is preparing a place for forgiven people! This is so true in John 14:3–6.

We receive forgiveness when we receive His free gift (1 John 2:1–2). Our God is full of mercy and forgiveness to all who come by the way of Jesus (Ephesians 2:4–5).

The world so needs to hear this truth. I wonder—would it have made a difference in the man who committed suicide if he had known this? It's too late to tell him now. But there is still time with a world that has opened its mind and heart to the enemy. Let's scale the wall of reality with the hope of Christ's atonement.

ASSIGNMENTS FOR THE WEEK

DAY 1
Read Joshua 6 and answer the following questions:

- Would you have obeyed God's unusual battle plan without questions? Explain.

- Why did God want Israel to do battle in this unusual way?

DAY 2
Read Joshua 7 and answer the following questions:

- Why did other people have to die for the sins of one man? Explain.

- How hard is it to determine why God sometimes removes His blessings from us?

DAY 3
Read Joshua 8 and answer the following questions:

- The Bible says in verse 10 that Joshua "mustered the people." Why did he have to do this?

- Is it hard to try again when you have failed before? Explain.

DAY 4

Read Joshua 9 and answer the following questions:

- Why were Joshua and the elders so easily deceived? Why are we so easily deceived by our enemy?

- What are the tactics our enemy uses today to destroy hope within us?

DAY 5

Read Joshua 10 and answer the following questions:

- Why is it that the enemy fights us harder and with more strength when we sell out to God? We see this truth when five kings band together. Explain.

- What miracle do you need in your present wall-scaling moment? Share it with your group.

STUDY 13

Sundays in America
Focal Text: Numbers 15:30-41

The year was 1610. For the first time in American history, in the colony of Virginia the "Blue Law" was adopted. This law was also called the "Sunday Law." It said the following:

> Every man and woman shall repair in the morning to the divine service and sermons preached upon the Sabbath day, and in the afternoon to divine service, and catechizing, upon pain for the first fault to lose their provision and the allowance for the whole week following; for the second, to lose the said allowance and also be whipt; and for the third to suffer death.

This law sought to help those in the colonies to be faithful to the fourth commandment, Exodus 20:8–11.

This law is still on the books in some states today. It was said that newly elected president George Washington was once stopped as he was headed from Connecticut to New York to worship on Sunday. He was severely chastised and had to promise that he was going directly to church. Brothers and sisters, it is impossible and even ridiculous to attempt to convince people to worship against their will.

Consider our day. We live in a time when fewer and fewer Americans are attending worship services. On any given Sunday there are more Americans who are not in church than there are who are in church. Religious leaders have over and over researched the question of why this is taking place. Here are a few findings from their research: People are working so much that Sunday is their only day to rest. People are so overworked and behind that they need Sunday to catch up, and people are disenchanted with organized church.

Here are the excuses I have heard in the last year: "I'm too busy." "I'm so tired." "We've gotten distracted." "We've gotten out of the habit." "Why should I?"

In Numbers 15 Moses writes about a familiar scene to Americans. Here is the scene—it is the Sabbath day, the day of which God has said, "Set aside this day for me." The people were commanded to do no work on this day. But on this particular day, as the camp worshiped, rested, and reflected, a man was spotted picking up sticks (vv. 32–36,)

The people were in shock. This had never happened before. In their two years of following the commandments of

God, no one had ever dared break the Sabbath laws. But even worse, here was a guy who seemed to do it both openly and defiantly. The people took him into custody and asked the Lord, "What should we do here?"

Now this was not the story of a man who was freezing in the desert and needed fire to survive. This was not the story of a man who was starving and needed to cook food to survive. Duguid writes, "This man does this in front of two million people. Did he think no one would see the fire? No, hardly. He brazenly went out in front of everyone and broke God's definite law. This had to be dealt with or the whole community would be compromised" (Duguid, 192).

Brothers and sisters, was this the first time this had taken place? Or maybe the better question would be "Why did Moses place this story here?" I think the verses before us give us a clue to the answer to the second question.

In the previous verses Moses has been writing specifically about sin and how sin is atoned for. When God's people sinned, there was atonement offered when repentance occurred (see chapter 12). But in verses 30–31 we read how the people were to deal with someone who sinned willfully. This person opposes God in defiance. This person despises and reviles God. He or she openly and without repentance breaks the commandments of God. To such a person there is zero forgiveness offered because there is no remorse for sin. The sin is still ongoing.

I imagine the man as being one who had been breaking God's commands all along. But now his heart had become so hard that he was openly defying God. This man had come to a point of no return. By our own choice, Jesus says, we can blaspheme the Holy Spirit.

So what should be done with such a person? God directed the nation to stone him as a testimony of what the end result is when disobeying God. There was too much on the line to let this go.

We fast-forward in time to Acts 5, when the church was in her beginning days. A similar scene was taking place. This time a man and his wife were sinning against God: they had lied to God, and they had lied to people. What happened to the couple? They both died under the hand of God's judgment.

One needs to pay close attention here: Gane writes, "Defiance of God is often the sin that tips a person over the edge of rebellion" (Gane, 626).

So are all Americans over the edge of rebellion who are not attending church? It depends on the intention of the person missing church. If it is for sickness, the answer is no. If it is for just not wanting to attend, maybe yes and in many cases a definite yes. If it is a result of hating God, you know the obvious answer.

But there is good news in the reality of a world in rebellion. God offers forgiveness for all who genuinely repent. The truth is—no animal sacrifice can atone for such sin. No amount of church attendance can atone for sin. It is only the blood of Jesus Christ that can atone for our sin. This is why John 3:16 has become the reality of all who love to worship the Lord on the Lord's day.

ASSIGNMENTS FOR THE WEEK

DAY 1

Read Joshua 11–12 and answer the following questions:

- What would have happened to God's army
  if the people had decided no longer to obey God?

- How is the church compared to God's army,
  and how important is it for the army to be
  united? Explain.

DAY 2

Read Joshua 13–14 and answer the following questions:

- What would happen if God's people failed to
  conquer the rest of the land? What did happen?

- Why did God leave Caleb alive all these
  years? Explain.

DAY 3

Read Joshua 15–19 and answer the following questions:

- What is God's reward for all who obey Him?

- What is God's judgment for those who do
  not obey Him?

DAY 4

Read Joshua 20 and answer the following questions:

- What were the cities of refuge?

- Why were they so important for people who failed?
  Where is our city of refuge?

DAY 5

Read Joshua 21–22 and answer the following questions:

- What would it have felt like to have been able to go
  home after you completed your tour of duty?

- What should we do when there is sin in the
  church? Give reasons.

STUDY 14

Going Too Far
Focal Text: Numbers 16

W hen I first sat down with my new friend, it was clear he had something deep within his heart. He began the conversation by saying, "Brother Keith, the man went too far." I had no clue who or what he was referring to. But by the end of our conversation, he had told me the sad story of how his friendship with a brother had deteriorated to the point that his friend took him by the hand and prayed the following: "Dear Lord, strike dead whichever one of us is wrong."

How could it be possible for two brothers in Christ to come to this place? This is the reality of life in a broken world. In this week's devotion we see this same issue happening during Israel's days of wandering in the wilderness. Take a moment and read verses 1– 3.

We are not sure of the exact date of this confrontation, but we are sure of its validity—because this is God's Word and also because this is far too common in our lives. I can see Moses coming out of his tent to see the sun rising. To his surprise he sees a large crowd approaching him. He is familiar with the crowd. He knows the leaders. One of the leaders is a Levite and the other two are from the tribe of Reuben.

I can hear Moses greeting the rest of the group, who were, by the way, his chosen leaders in the camp. These were his teammates, his friends, and his brothers. Were these men coming to pray with him? Was there a problem where he could help?

Suddenly the moment becomes intense as the crowd is hostile in their looks. What has happened with these men? In shock, Moses hears them as they begin making accusations against him. It was as if a time bomb were going off in Moses's heart. These brothers accuse Moses of going too far in his leadership.

As we dig deeper we discover that these men are not concerned for the glory of God. They are not concerned for Moses's health, and they are not concerned about the congregation. These men were blinded by the green-eyed monster of envy and jealousy.

Moses is accused of thinking of himself better than the rest of the congregation. He is accused of leading the people without God's approval. Brothers and sisters, we have each been in this place, when a friendship has exploded because of the green-eyed monster of envy and jealously. I have been on both sides of the explosion.

At the times when I have been the match-lighter in the explosion, I have had to repent before God and then before my friend (James 4:1–10). If this is you today, take the road of repentance. The other road is the road these men took with Moses, a road that will cost you your life in the end.

As we move our way through this chapter, I find myself examining Moses's responses very closely because I need to know how to correctly walk through such moments. My friend who cried before me was at the beginning of a long road that would take him through bitterness, anger, hatred, and regret before he arrived at the place where Moses was in Numbers 17.

Where was Moses in Numbers 17? We see where he was in verse 4. Moses takes a humble position. This humble position led him to handle this time-bomb moment correctly. Notice I did not say that he was perfect—he was far from perfect. We see Moses in the text getting very angry at one point. But his anger did not last very long.

Moses confronted the sin of this group. These men were listening to their own press about who they were (vv. 8–11). They were giving in to the dreaded sin of entitlement. These men thought they were worthy of occupying a great seat of influence in their nation. This viewpoint of entitlement put them at odds with the man of God.

The men came to the place where they did not even want to talk to Moses. They blamed him for all the troubles in the camp, which led to Moses's one moment of anger.

Here we see God teaching Moses a lesson about love. God tells him that He is about to destroy all the people. Moses cries out for mercy on them because he realizes that not everyone deserves to pay the price for the sin of these men.

What a picture we have of Christ, who was coming to take the place of humanity, who all deserve to die for their sins (1 Peter 3:18)! Moses warns the people of God's judgment on the offenders. Pay attention, brothers and sisters, to what happens to this group. The men are swallowed up in the earth. They go down to the pit. They perish from the land of the living.

Please reread the words above. Do your relationships ever deteriorate to the point that you wish this on those who are no longer your friends? Please do not read beyond this without working through it. The very next day Moses would have to deal with the same time bomb with the entire congregation.

As long as we live in a broken world, we will face the possibility of deteriorating friendships. Many of you are facing these truths as you read this. The question we need to ask is this: "How should I respond based on what I have read?" Moses takes no fewer than six steps in this process. I will be able only to list them along with their corresponding verses to amplify the point. I trust you will read each and apply them in your experience of being in friendships that sometimes go too far:

1. Moses exalts God alone (Psalm 34:3).

2. Moses is still before God (Psalm 46:10).

3. Moses humbles himself (1 Peter 5:6).

4. Moses trusts in what God is doing
   (2 Corinthians 10:6).

5. Moses trusts in God's power (2 Corinthians 10:7).

6. Moses loves those who count him as their
   enemy (Romans 12:14–21).

I pray you and I learn from these six steps that Moses took. Do not be discouraged when these are hard at first. Be patient and be persistent. God will overcome in His timing.

ASSIGNMENTS FOR THE WEEK

DAY 1

Read 2 Corinthians 1 and answer the following questions:

- Describe the comfort we need from God when we go through broken relationships.

- What promises has God given us as we go through these moments?

DAY 2

Read 2 Corinthians 2 and answer the following questions:

- How difficult is it to forgive someone who has hurt you? Explain.

- Why does Paul insist we reaffirm our love for an offender? Explain.

DAY 3

Read 2 Corinthians 3 and answer the following questions:

- Whom did Paul find sufficiency in, and whom do you find sufficiency in? Explain.

- Explain how God brings us to a spirit of liberty.

DAY 4

Read 2 Corinthians 4 and answer the following questions:

- Are you ever tempted to push your own views instead of seeking God's answer in your broken relationships? Why do we do this? Explain both answers.

- Explain what Paul means by "We do not lose heart" (v. 1).

DAY 5

Read 2 Corinthians 5 and answer the following questions:

- What hope is there for relationships in which one friend dies before the circumstance is resolved?

- What is the "ministry of reconciliation"? How do we apply this to broken relationships? Explain.

STUDY 15

My Apostate Gland
Focal Text: Numbers 17:1-13

When Roy Gane's father served as a pastor in New Jersey in the 1990s, he visited a man in the hospital who looked up and informed him, "Pastor, it's my apostate gland" (Gane, 649).

When I read this illustration, I knew I wanted to title this week's devotion "My Apostate Gland." Do you have an apostate gland? I must make this confession: I have one. Now this may come as a shock to you, but so do you. This crazy term is simply a way to illustrate our sin nature.

Certainly you have heard of "the sin nature." You and I inherited this nature at birth. It comes to us from Adam, and we pass it on to those who come behind us. Some people refer to this as simply "original sin." Grudem calls it "original pollution." We find clear references to this in Psalm 51:1–4; 58:3; and in Ephesians 2:3. We enter life with no spiritual life, and we have no natural bend to do what is right before God.

When Moses followed the call of God to lead the people of Israel from bondage to blessing, they came out with their "apostate glands." This truth has brought such insight to my daily life as a leader of people. It is no wonder these people were always acting in such a dysfunctional way toward God and His chosen leaders. In spite of all God had done for them, they still did not trust Him. Gane writes, "These people were damaged from the start. The brutal experience of bondage in Egypt made it difficult for them to rise above their preoccupation with basic physical survival" (Gane, 648).

In spite of all God's work in liberating them, loving them through provision of needs, and even consistent patience, it was not enough for them. They still withheld trust, and they still operated with the "apostate gland" of survival.

We could choose to look back to any of the chapters we have covered in the past, and we would see their sin nature at work. It was at work in chapter 11 when the people were described as "rabble." In chapter 14 their "apostate glands" led them to rebel against God. This rebellion would cost them the next forty years. It was at work in 16:41–50. Here in chapter 17 we still see it still at work.

At every step on the journey Israel complained. Moses said of these people in Deuteronomy 9:7, "From the day you came out of the land of Egypt until you came to this place, you have been rebellious against the Lord." Question: Would you have grown weary of such people?

But wait a minute—what about you and me? We also have this "apostate gland" inside us. Take a moment and look in the mirror. Do you see yourself clearly or are there things at work in you that you do not even realize are there? I hope you will take the time and have the courage not only to own up to having the gland but also to take out the gland.

In chapter 17 God does the one thing He could do with rebellious people. He sets up a miracle moment in which he does three things that point us to hope as people who have "apostate glands":

1. God proves who were the chosen leaders for His people.

Moses asks for the staffs of the twelve heads of the tribes of Israel. Moses had carried a staff and had been told to wave it across the Red Sea. The sea parted in Exodus 14. The power was not in the staff but simply represented the vested authority given.

Each leader gives his staff to Moses after placing his name on it. Aaron does the same with his. The Lord says, "Whoever's staff I cause to sprout is my chosen leader." One day later it is Aaron's staff that has not only sprouted but has also put forth buds, produced blossoms, and borne ripe almonds in a twenty-four-hour period.

Aaron is God's chosen leader to be the priest for the people. Moses takes the staff and places it before the altar as a constant reminder of who God's leader is. Brothers and sisters, it is the cross that has become our reminder of who our priest to God is.

2. God is pointing all of humanity to their need of a true leader.

Aaron's staff had no power of its own. At one point it was a part of an almond tree. But the tree had to be cut down and die before it could become a staff. There was no life in the staff. But when God touched it, it gave forth life.

This is the miracle of our connection to Jesus. In John 15:2 He said, "Every branch in me that does not bear fruit he takes away." Life comes to all who are in Christ. Life comes forth from Jesus (Romans 8:11). He alone is the author of life. He alone has all authority in which you can trust. He alone gives you the ability to live a Christian life that bears fruit. "You did not choose me, but I chose you and appointed you that you should go and bear fruit and that your fruit should abide" (John 15:16).

God will break the power of our "apostate glands." He will render them ineffective by giving us His life (Ephesians 2:4–5; John 8:31–36). Our task is to confess our "apostate glands," repent of them, and embrace the great power of God. This is what Jesus describes in John 15:1–17.

3. God was patient with His people, and He is patient with us.

Israel would experience God's patience in meeting her needs for forty years in the wilderness. What is tragic is simply that this generation would die and another one would have to come before the blessing of victory would come.

God does not want this for your life nor does He want this for my life. The question is "What do you and I want for our lives?" Personally, I have allowed my "apostate gland" to lead long enough. It's time to overcome by the blood of Jesus.

This week you will continue to read through 2 Corinthians, where Paul is writing to a church with an over-abundance of "apostate glands."

ASSIGNMENTS FOR THE WEEK

DAY 1

Read 2 Corinthians 6 and answer the following questions:

- Why do we sometimes put off dealing with the sins we know are present?

- Why did people treat Paul so terribly, and why did he have to go through so much suffering? Explain.

DAY 2

Read 2 Corinthians 7 and answer the following questions:

- Describe the process of cleansing oneself.

- Are you living with regret for confronting someone in his or her sin, or are you living in regret for a past sin? Describe how one can overcome this.

DAY 3

Read 2 Corinthians 8 and answer the following questions:

- How could our "apostate glands" rob us from the joy of giving? Explain.

- Did Jesus possess an "apostate gland"? Defend your answer.

DAY 4

Read 2 Corinthians 9 and answer the following questions:

- Have you ever wanted to do something but your "apostate gland" got in the way? Explain how it felt.

- How does giving bring joy to a Christian's life?

DAY 5

Read 2 Corinthians 10 and answer the following questions:

- How does a believer walk in the flesh but wage war in the Spirit?

- Why should we boast in the Lord? Why does this aid in destroying the "apostate gland"?

STUDY 16

Those Who Save Lives
Focal Text: Numbers 18–19

As I begin writing this chapter, I am sitting in the car next to Sherry, who is driving this leg of our journey home from a time of great sorrow. Her fifty-three-year-old brother was suddenly called home by the Father. I could never write words on a page that would describe how we feel this morning as we silently drive home.

Certainly many of you can identify with the shock of getting the phone call that was your worst nightmare. Often in these moments we second-guess the process, including questioning God for the "why" of sudden death. It is in these circumstances that as Christ-followers we must keep truth in perspective so that we do not sorrow as the world does. We are people who are filled with hope because we serve a God who eternally saves lives.

Sherry and I are eternally thankful that Stanley did not "perish."

You may ask, "What is this 'perish' business you refer to?" In the Bible the word *perish* refers to dying and spending eternity in hell. I pray this truth leaps off the page and into your heart. This word was used by the Israelites (Numbers 17:13) to describe the reason for their fear before God. Israel knew God was holy, and whether she wanted to admit it or not, she was unholy. On her best day Israel could not stand before God alone.

This is why Israel cried out for someone who could keep them from perishing. This was not their first time to feel this way. When God met with Moses at Mount Sinai, the people cried out to Moses, "You speak to God for us." They wanted Moses to be their mediator. But now two years later, they again have come to realize that they need someone to stand in their place.

This is why we have Numbers 18–19 before us. Here we read of God both providing leaders and picturing a leader who was to come.

In Numbers 18 we read that God provided leaders to be the mediators for the people. We know these leaders to be from the tribe of Levi. The Levite tribe had placed upon them tremendous responsibilities.

God had put before the people the proper way in which they were to approach Him, described in Leviticus. Before this moment the entire congregation would pay a price for the improper approach to the tabernacle. Now the Levites would bear the burden if they failed to approach God correctly or if they allowed the people to approach incorrectly. Gane writes, "Whether the people are far or near to the Holy of Holies, the leaders must take seriously their responsibility to mediate for the people" (Gane, 653).

This is so near to my heart today because my brother-in-law was so faithful as an elder in his church. He lived a life of excellence in leading people to Jesus as director of their camping ministry. It was his greatest desire to see everyone come to Jesus. I honor him today as one who saved lives, because he pointed them to Jesus.

Are there people who could be considered saviors in your life in this way? If so, pay attention to what is written in Numbers 18.

Much of chapter 18 is dominated by the people's responsibility in providing for those who led them well. I can say of the people I pastor, they care for me far more than I deserve. I want to challenge you to reach out to your spiritual leaders this week. I am sure they would be encouraged by your kindness to them.

As we come to chapter 19 we see the picture of a leader who was to come. For many this chapter seems so beyond understanding. Here we see a red heifer being burned outside the camp so that the sins of the people might be covered. This pictures for us the work of our one true Savior, who is Jesus, who was crucified outside the city (Hebrews 13:12). This Savior gave His life in our place so that we could go free (Hebrews 9:11–14).

How could we read this chapter without truly seeing the picture before us? Unlike the red heifer, which could only cover sin, Jesus removed our sin debt. Unlike the red heifer, which would have his kin-folk killed next year and every year after, Jesus died once for all (Hebrews 7:24–26).

This truth leads us to give thanks for those who lead us well and for the One they are pointing us to.

But all this theology is useless unless we can scale the wall of reality when we suddenly lose a loved one to death. Many people live in fear about where their loved one is after death. Others fear death because they do not have a firm hold on where they themselves will be in eternity.

For both groups I offer you the truth of God's Word, which scales the wall of reality when death comes. "This is good, and it is pleasing in the sight of God our Savior, who desires all people to be saved and to come to the knowledge of the truth. For there is one God, and there is one mediator between God and men, the man Christ Jesus, who gave himself as a ransom for all" (1 Timothy 2:3–6).

When Sherry and I stood at the casket housing the body of her brother Stanley, we wept because we loved him, we would miss him, and we hurt for his family. But very soon our tears were replaced with tears of joy, because we knew Stanley had already been saved from his last enemy, which is death.

How can I do anything less than praise the Lord as we drive down the road to our ministry field? The words of

Scripture flow through my mind this day: "Thanks be to God, who gives us victory through our Lord Jesus Christ" (1 Corinthians 15:57).

This week allow God's Word to help you scale the reality of living a life in victory—knowing you have a Savior!

ASSIGNMENTS FOR THE WEEK

DAY 1
Read 2 Corinthians 11 and answer the following questions:

- What are the simple things of the gospel that are often overlooked by people in times of trial?

- Should pastors be paid to minister or should they not? Explain.

DAY 2
Read 2 Corinthians 12 and answer the following questions:

- Give an example of how God's grace has been sufficient in your life as a Christ-follower.

- What was Paul's "thorn in the flesh"? Defend your answer.

DAY 3
Read 2 Corinthians 13 and answer the following questions:

- Why is it important for all believers to test themselves to see if they are in the faith?

- Who are the leaders who have pointed you to the Savior? Take time to pray for them today.

DAY 4

Read Revelation 20–21 and answer the following questions:

- Why does the Lord have to judge the lost people of the world?

- What are the things about heaven you look forward to experiencing?

DAY 5

Read Psalm 116 and answer the following questions:

- How precious are God's people in His sight? Explain.

- What extent did God go to in order to prove how precious we are to Him? Explain.

STUDY 17

A Bad Place
Focal Text: Numbers 20:1-10

It had been several years since I had heard anything about a former pastor friend. I was blessed to be in this friend's hometown on a ministry engagement. I met his father one night before the service where I was preaching and asked about my friend. His response was heartbreaking: "He is in a bad place."

The truth is that this pastor knew much about the theology of God, but there came a moment when his reality was stronger than his belief in God. Question: Could there ever be such a bad place where you would be tempted to turn away from what you believed?

This week we find Moses in a bad place. Forty years of wandering in the desert under the judgment of God had been completed. Moses's faith in God was strong. The Lord had been so faithful to him and his people. Since the first day in the desert (Exodus 3), Moses had not been perfect, but he had been faithful.

On this day recorded in Numbers 20, Moses returns to Kadesh, the very place where the people rebelled against God forty years earlier (Numbers 13–14). We see him coming to a bad place. It is a place where his emotions become the wall that theology needs to scale to the top.

Notice the following concerning Moses's emotions:

- **Moses's emotions are torn.**

As Moses stood in Kadesh, the forty years of desert life must have been going through his mind. As he looked at his weather-torn hands, he saw the wear of leading complaining people. As he stood there, he had performed more funerals than any man in the history of the world. He is at least 120 years old. It was a bad place.

- **Moses's emotions are further torn.**

His godly sister, Miriam, has died. We remember those early months of Moses's life when she helped save him from Pharaoh (Exodus 2:4–10). She was a true worshiper of God, even though she was far from perfect. Moses's heart must have broken to see his sister leave the world.

- **Moses's emotions were now at the tipping point.**

It was time for the people to go in to the promised land. Verse 2 begins with the word *now*. If you have followed the story line of Numbers, you knew there would be a *now*. The people came to Moses because they did not have water. This is the same old grieving story. God had been faithful in every moment of their lives, but with each new crisis they forgot the love of God. Emotions have a way of robbing us of truth.

The congregation blamed Moses and Aaron. This time they accused Moses and Aaron of leading the people into a death trap. Again, it's the same old story. I don't know if you see it or not, but I see the devil's handprints all over this emotionally charged scene.

The people labeled the location as "this evil place" (v. 5). The Hebrew word speaks of a broken and spoiled place, a place that is not easy. The NLT translates the word as "terrible."

When Moses's emotions were at a tipping point, they came to an "evil place." Are you in this same place today, or do you have a friend in such a place? Hear the warning of God's Word: be careful about your decisions when you are in a bad place (1 Peter 5:6–8).

Moses knew exactly what to do with his emotions. In verse 6 he went before the Lord. As it had been so many times before, God came down in His glory veiled behind a cloud.

Take a moment and read God's directions to Moses: "Take the staff, and assemble the congregation, you and Aaron your brother, and tell the rock before their eyes to yield its water" (v. 8).

Pay close attention now. Does God know all things? If He does, then why does He not calm Moses's emotions?

As we read God's response to Moses, we must understand who God is and the relationship God has with Moses. From the first day in the desert (Exodus 3) God has been Moses's "rock" to lean on. In Deuteronomy 32:4 Moses speaks of God as his "rock." He is the rock on which Moses could place the full weight of his emotions (Psalm 18:1–2).

But instead of standing on the rock, Moses makes a bad decision in this "bad place."

- **Moses's emotions take over.**

In anger Moses refers to his congregation as "rebels." The word speaks of a bitter and disobedient people. The fact is, this is the second generation Moses has led. Surely he knew who they were. This was not his first rodeo.

But the emotions of anger, frustration, and pride swell up and break out in Moses. Moses strikes the rock in defiance of God's direct command. Notice that as the water of God's grace comes rushing out so that the nation's water needs are met, all seems to be okay. Who can blame Moses? All of us have those moments when our emotions get the best of us.

But wait! Did we hear God correctly? Moses has lost his second-chance opportunity to enter the promised land? Is God being unfair with Moses? In this moment the wall of reality seems far too high for any person to scale. How often have our emotional outbursts gotten us into far more trouble than we thought we deserved? How often have we blamed God for what seemed to be cruel and unusual punishment for our failure?

In this place either we can just accept what happened or we can attempt to scale the wall of reality. Let's scale the wall together.

Numbers 27:14 helps us to understand why God was so severe in his judgment of Moses. What Moses did was considered a rebellious act of breaking faith with God. Gane writes, "To strike the rock, Moses lifted his hand, which held his staff. This language suggests he is sinning with a high hand. He is being defiant toward God. He was saying to the people, I am in charge" (Gane, 671–72).

If God allowed Moses to act this way, it would be setting the precedent for the people's continual emotional outbursts of trying to take away God's holy and sovereign reign.

Be assured: God takes His holiness and our obedience very seriously. Moses lost much because of his sin. But God's eternal grace was sufficient because Moses accepted God's judgment, and he got to see the promised land (but did not enter it) before he died. When Moses died, God took him to the eternal promised land, called heaven, because he still trusted in the Rock, who is Jesus (1 Corinthians 10:4).

This very day you may have emotionally lost it. If you have, confess your sin to God. Receive His forgiveness and stand on the rock of Christ's forgiveness.

This week find encouragement from the writings of a fellow emotional disciple, Peter, who often kept his foot in his mouth in his early years of ministry.

ASSIGNMENTS FOR THE WEEK

DAY 1

Read 1 Peter 1 and answer the following questions:

- How does the devil lead us to lose sight of "our eternal hope"? Give an illustration.

- Peter urges toward "preparing your minds for action" in verse 13. Describe what this means.

DAY 2

Read 1 Peter 2 and answer the following questions:

- Why is Jesus called the "living stone"? Describe what happens when people stumble over the "living stone."

- How does Christ's example help us with our emotions in the day-to-day life issues we face?

DAY 3

Read 1 Peter 3 and answer the following questions:

- What are the typical emotions experienced in a family? What are the typical emotions experienced in a single person's household?

- How can God use your standing on the "rock of Jesus" to be a life witness to those who are in a bad place?

DAY 4

Read 1 Peter 4 and answer the following questions:

- How does knowing that we will give an account to Jesus help us in directing our emotions?

- What does it mean when Peter directs us to "entrust [our] souls to a faithful Creator"?

DAY 5

Read 1 Peter 5 and answer the following questions:

- How emotionally hard must it be for pastors to lead emotional people? Who is there for a pastor? Explain.

- Describe how Peter teaches us to combat the attacks of the enemy.

STUDY 18

Fighting to Get Out: Part 1
Focal Text: Numbers 20:11–21:35

It happens from time to time even though I do not want to admit it. What happens? I find myself getting frustrated with myself. Let me explain. I want to repair something that is broken in our bathroom. I carefully watch the YouTube video. I buy the needed parts, and I have the correct tools. But for some reason I cannot seem to repair the broken piece like the person in the video. Brothers and sisters, this is frustrating.

Sometimes I believe we as Christ-followers find ourselves spiritually in the same position. We realize something is broken. We read God's Word for the answer. We walk the steps outlined in God's Word. But for some reason it does not work for us.

I could use personal illustrations here from people I have had the joy of pastoring. But for integrity's sake I will write only in general terms. Many dysfunctional parents will try to right the ship by walking the steps and it does not work out. Many people can't live in the present because they are locked in the death grip of a hurt from the past. Day after day and year after year they fail in the battle. Each new year begins with high hopes of the year being different. Commitments are made, but nothing changes because for some reason the Bible seems not to be working—or could it be some other reason?

For forty long years the nation of Israel had been fighting to get out, but she could not. We know the reasons she could not get out. But now things were about to change. I hope they are about to change for you.

The people of Israel were about to discover how to fight their way out of failure, loss, and defeat. As we look at the true narrative of their lives over the next two chapters, we are going to discover four faith-building truths that will help us fight our way out. But before we look at the text, I want to give you a quote from 1 Timothy 6:12: "Fight the good fight of faith" (KJV).

Say those words with me: *Fight the good fight of faith.*

As the dust settles from Moses's bad moment (Numbers 20:1–13), the narrative moves forward quickly. In verses 14–21 we discover our first faith-building truth:

I. If you are going to be free, you will have to fight through dysfunction in your family.

If you had a map of that day, you would see that Moses was desiring to take the closest route to the promised land. The route would take his people through the nation belonging to close relatives. We know them to be the Edomites. They were the descendants of Esau, cousins of the Israelites, who were descendants of Jacob, Esau's brother.

To our shock the people say, "No, you cannot cross our nation." Wow! How could this be? Had not their cousins been through enough in over four hundred years of captivity in Egypt? What's the deal?

This could not have been revenge, because Jacob and Esau had made peace before they died (Genesis 32–33). Had they spent all these years consumed by themselves? A closer look at Scripture (Obadiah 1) reveals that these people did not like their cousins. This was truly family dysfunction.

Many who read this today have been trapped in things like this for years. Let me tell you: you must forgive the past and free yourself from people who will not forgive the past. Jesus taught us to take the high road (Mark 10:42–45).

If your heart is saying, "I can't wait for the day I can get even," be assured that you are in bondage. Paul taught us to respond in the totally opposite way (Romans 12:14–21). The truth is that God was leading Israel in a great path. He is sovereign over everything. Where He was taking Israel, they had no room for suitcases filled with dysfunction. Follow Israel's example: she simply turned and walked away.

II. If you are going to be free, you will have to work through the departures of others.

The verses that follow (20:22–29) tell us the story of the departure of Aaron from this life. Moses and Aaron had started this mission together over forty years earlier. Now Aaron was dying. He had made mistakes, but God was gracious in placing his son to be the successor as high priest for Israel.

Here is a hard fact of ministry: not everyone who starts with you in ministry will finish with you.

Sometimes leaders die and we mourn. Sometimes leaders are called to another ministry and we mourn. Still at other times they fail miserably and have to leave. In these moments we also mourn. The nation mourned thirty days for Aaron, but then they moved forward.

We need to learn well the faith-building truth of whom we look to alone. We look to Jesus, who is the author and finisher of our faith (Hebrews 12:2). I believe it is time that you fight through the departures in your life. Heed these words: Look up, get up, and go on in Jesus's name.

III. If you are going to be free you will have to walk back through places of defeat.

The narrative in the book of Numbers moves into chapter 21. The new generation of Israel knew about this place. Certainly their parents would have told them about the day (Numbers 14:42–45) when the Amalekites and the Canaanites, living in the Negev, had pushed them completely out of the path they were trying to walk in.

Forty years earlier God had used these people as His agents of judgment. But now their crimes had caught up with them. I want you to grasp this truth: God always takes us back to the old battlefields where He intended for us to have a different ending. God does not intend for you to end your life in defeat.

The nation cried out to God for His hand to be on them. God listened to their cries and gave them the victory because they were now in a place of obedience. God will always say yes to requests that are in His will (1 John 5:13–14).

This was the nation's first victory erasing the failure of the past. Are there fields in your past where there is a white flag of surrender? Isn't it time you pick up the banner of the cross and go back there and claim it for Jesus?

Wow! This is a lot to take in and these are steps we need to take seriously. Say the words with me again: *Fight the good fight of faith.*

In the next chapter we will walk through the fourth faith-building truth that will lead us to win the victory in the places where we have been in bondage. This week we will be in Proverbs together, digging out truth that will help us walk the steps of faith.

ASSIGNMENTS FOR THE WEEK

DAY 1

Read Proverbs 1–2 and answer the following questions:

- What is the fear of the Lord and how does this fear place us on the path of wisdom?

- How would treasuring God's wisdom in your mind help you with family conflict?

DAY 2

Read Proverbs 3–4 and answer the following questions:

- How are we to live our lives in our families before our neighbors?

- Why should we be careful to ponder the path of our feet?

DAY 3

Read Proverbs 12–14 and answer the following questions:

- How does righteousness deliver us from death? Focus your answer around the death that comes to many families.

- Explain why the wrong way seems to be the right way when we are faced with challenges.

DAY 4

- **Read Proverbs 16–18 and answer the following questions:**

  - How does our speech contribute to the health of our relationships?

  - Why is a dry morsel of bread with peace better than a house full of feasting with strife? Explain how you would help a person to come to peace in his or her home life.

DAY 5

Read Proverbs 19–21 and answer the following questions:

- How does discipline aid in the growth of a healthy family? Give reasons.

- Why do the issues in our hearts seem so hard to talk about? Focus on 20:5 in your search for the answer.

STUDY 19

Fighting to Get Out: Part 2
Focal Text: Numbers 20:11–21:35

It had been so long since I had seen this person. I had known this individual years earlier and honestly was even surprised the person was still alive. The life this acquaintance was living all those years ago was headed toward certain destruction.

This individual was born in a dysfunctional family and early in life had embraced the dysfunction as a normal way of life. Year after year it was the same: one broken relationship had led to another broken relationship. A journey through this person's past would be like walking on the battle field of Normandy Beach after the battle of D-Day. Certainly this individual could not get out of these life circumstances.

But as I stood there, the person looked totally different. I could not hold back my question. I asked, "What has happened in your life?" With tears, the acquaintance responded, "I met Jesus."

As we come back to our studies in the book of Numbers, we see a people who have spent the last forty years in the wilderness of God's judgment. Now they are fighting to get out of where they are. With each step of their journey, faith is building.

Just as with my friend who placed faith in Jesus, you and I are called to put our faith in Jesus. This is the only way you and I can get out of the fight we are in. In our last chapter I gave you a challenge from 1 Timothy 6:12. Here is the challenge: "Fight the good fight of faith" (KJV).

This new generation of believers had to fight their way out of the past. To accomplish this, there would be four faith-building truths that would help them fight their way out by faith. Here are the three we discovered together in our last chapter:

1. You have to walk through dysfunction in your family.

2. You have to walk through the departures of others.

3. You have to walk back through places of defeat.

Here is the fourth faith-building truth:

4. You have to embrace by faith your defining moments.

With their first victory firmly in hand the people began moving forward, but very quickly they became impatient.

The King James Version uses the word *discouraged*. Question: Does impatience lead to discouragement or does discouragement lead to impatience? I believe discouragement leads to impatience. The people were discouraged with God and how He was providing for them. In their discouragement they became tired of waiting for what He had promised.

Even though all the blessings of the best food and water were just down the road, the people of God could not wait because they had the wrong viewpoint of God and God's will. When we come to defining moments we must have a different viewpoint than the world. The world sees the glass as half-empty. The world consistently complains about what they do not possess, and they consistently blame God for the problems in the world.

Suddenly God sends judgment upon the people. Fiery snakes come out of nowhere and begin biting people. The word *fiery* speaks about a snake with venom that felt like fire. "Perhaps some snakes will help them appreciate His bread" (Gane, 687).

Brothers and sisters, what a scene it must have been as people were being bitten and people were dying! Now we see complaining people becoming repentant people. Consider this fact: Often God places us in defining moments to change our viewpoints of life.

First Corinthians 10:11 teaches us how these things happened to Israel for the purpose of becoming our examples. So what do we gain from this example?

Let's keep reading the text. Moses cries out to God for the people. God instructs Moses to make a serpent out of bronze, and he is to place it on a pole. The people who were bitten were instructed to look at the serpent and they would be healed.

Be assured that God was not pointing the people to mysticism. This was not magic. It was symbolic of two things: First, "to look at the serpent was to admit one's sin and its result. This was their confession" (Gane, 680).

Second, many years later Jesus would be speaking with a Pharisee and would say, "As Moses lifted up the serpent in the wilderness, so must the Son of Man be lifted up, that whoever believes in Him may have eternal life" (John 3:14–15).

If we are going to fight our way out of where we are, our eyes must be on Jesus. It is Christ alone who brings victory to our lives.

Once the dust settles from this changing viewpoint, the people move forward (Numbers 21:10-20. Here we discover another defining moment. The people of God begin singing a song of victory to the Lord. As we come to defining moments, it is the song in our hearts that often carries us through. If you and I have songs of defeat within us, the victory cannot be ours. Psalm 95:6 directs us to "come, let us worship and bow down; let us kneel before the Lord, our Maker!"

God has called us to change our songs. When Jesus came to a defining moment in the wilderness in Luke 4, He won the victory. Here is what He said to Satan, who wanted Him to bow down and worship him: "You shall worship the Lord your God, and him only shall you serve" (Luke 4:8).

Worship fuels the way we do battle. It would be at the walls of Jericho (Joshua 6) where the people would experience the enemy's walls falling down as they shouted victory in Jesus!

The chapter ends with the nation edging their way to the promised land (vv. 21–35). In two major defining-moment battles, the victory comes. We can have different endings to our battles than we had in the past. God wants you, through Him, to defeat the enemy. God is willing to empower you to build a new life if you do it His way.

In Deuteronomy 6:18 Moses makes the above truth so clear: "And you shall do what is right and good in the sight of the Lord, that it may go well with you, and that you may go in and take possession of the good land that the Lord swore to give to your fathers."

The day had come. The people were now getting it right with God. This week I want to challenge you to walk the faith steps with God. But make sure you are right with God before you take the first step.

ASSIGNMENTS FOR THE WEEK

DAY 1
Read Psalm 27 and answer the following questions:

- How many years does a person need to serve the Lord before he or she can say with confidence, "I trust the Lord totally"? Explain.

- In verses 7–12 we are encouraged to pray. How does prayer help us in our faith moments? Give examples from your own life.

DAY 2
Read Psalm 29–30 and answer the following questions:

- How does worshiping the Lord give you confidence in your daily life of faith?

- How does Psalm 30 encourage us not to forget what God has already done for us?

DAY 3
Read Psalm 31 and answer the following questions:

- Why is it not always easy to place one's trials in God's hands? Explain.

- How much love do you have for God, and are there things that are keeping you from drawing closer to God?

DAY 4

Read Psalm 32 and answer the following questions:

- How hard is it to be courageous in our faith if we have sin in our lives?

- Describe what it feels like to be forgiven by God.

DAY 5

Read Psalm 33–34 and answer the following questions:

- Are there things you have asked God for over and over? Explain what God has taught you as you have waited on Him.

- How would you explain to someone his or her need of tasting to see if God is good? Defend your answer.

STUDY 20

Fighting an Unseen Enemy
Focal Text: Numbers 22

Chinese philosopher Sun Tzu is quoted as saying, "The supreme art of war is to subdue the enemy without fighting."

The reality of faith teaches us not only of God's provisions for victory over enemies we can see but also of the hidden reality of God's provisions for victory over enemies we cannot see. The apostle Paul wrote about such battles in Ephesians 6:10–13.

On our journey as Christ-followers from bondage to blessing there are many battles you and I know nothing about. These battles are fought for us, and they further our advance in faith without our even being aware of them. I believe one of the greatest praise gatherings we will have in heaven will be when we clearly see the battles the Lord fought on our behalf while we were on the earth.

We see an illustration of God fighting His people's battles in the life of Israel as she is battling her way into the promised land. Our focal text positions Israel closer and closer to the reality of what God has promised. Standing in the way is an enemy whom God has already said to leave alone (Deuteronomy 2:9). But the enemy does not know this. The king of Moab, whose nation is a descendant of Lot's daughter (Genesis 19:37–38), devises a plan for his nation to attack the people of God.

We realize there are several things driving this king: there is great fear in his heart; there is great distress as the nation finds itself in a difficult place; and finally, the forces of hell are pushing him toward war.

The elders, along with the king, come up with what they believe is a spiritual solution to their problem. The leaders want to hire Balaam, who is a diviner, to curse the nation of Israel. This is a pagan prophet who has a reputation for great spiritual power of both blessing and cursing. His services are very costly. Roy Gane comments, "If he is a polytheist, it appears that he would have dealt with whatever supernatural beings were relevant to the needs of his clients" (Gane, 690).

Here is an important point for us to grasp. All this is happening apart from the knowledge of God's people.

As we continue reading the unfolding story, there is a strange twist. This pagan prophet consults God. Yes, he consults the God of Israel (Yahweh). And an even greater twist occurs when God (Elohim) answers him with direction.

God tells Balaam *not* to go and curse Israel because He has already determined that they will be "blessed."

It is here where I want to point out three things about Balaam for your consideration:

1. Balaam *wants* the money from Balak, but God says no.

This pagan prophet is not happy about God's answer. He would rather curse them, but God forbids him. How many people would take advantage of us if they were only allowed to by God? How quickly would Satan dispose of us if only God would allow it?

2. Balaam is *tempted* by the offer of more money.

Basically Balak offers Balaam a blank check if he will only curse God's people. Deep inside Balaam wants this, but he knows God's power is greater than his.

Here we see the Lord telling Balaam to go with the leaders. Has God changed His mind? The answer is no. God is testing Balaam to see if his heart is obedient. Very quickly the story line makes it clear that Balaam does not want to obey God's will. He is going with the hopes of getting the money from the king.

3. Balaam *angers* God because of the intentions of his heart.

I believe God's anger is righteously directed at Balaam because he is headed to the king with hopes of getting the money. If God allowed him to go with his present mind-set, he would curse the people of Israel. Still yet, we must understand that the people of God have zero knowledge of the plot against them.

The angel of the Lord (a theophany of God) comes as the adversary of Balaam. Only the donkey sees the Lord before him. In kindness to her master, on three occasions she tries to protect him.

The supernatural continues to happen as the donkey is able to speak. "Unlike the serpent in Genesis 3, the donkey utters undeceptive words" (Gane, 695). Here we see God's great grace in stopping Balaam from his direction to certain destruction.

Brothers and sisters, how many times have you and I been graciously stopped by God's supernatural hand? God speaks directly to Balaam: "Your way is perverse before me" (Numbers 22:32). This prophet has in his heart a plan that would cause trouble for the people of God.

How could all of this be? We find our answer in 2 Peter 2:15–16: "Forsaking the right way, they have gone astray. They have followed the way of Balaam, the son of Beor, who loved gain from wrongdoing, but was rebuked for his own transgression; a speechless donkey spoke with human voice and restrained the prophet's madness."

This man was focused on his own gain. He was in madness, fighting the true and living God. This scene in the history of Israel speaks volumes to unseen battles in our day.

The Bible says in Acts 20:29 that "fierce wolves will come in among you, not sparing the flock. We live in a day filled with false teachers who have the same plan as Balaam (2 Peter 2; Revelation 2:14).

Such teachers teach falsely, focusing on our flesh so that we will fall prey to their trap of selfish gain. Such leaders have a terrible impact on our lives. Balaam had a devastating impact on Israel later in our story (Numbers 31).

What do we gain from this battle?

- For Balaam it was all about the money.
- For Satan it was all about destroying the people of God.
- For God it was all about destroying the works of Satan.

Here are three warnings for us as we face unseen battles: (1) Be careful about the people you follow. (2) Be careful about why you follow them. (3) Be careful with following the teaching of those who are false teachers

This week we will walk with Jeremiah as he faces the Balaams of his day.

ASSIGNMENTS FOR THE WEEK

DAY 1
Read Jeremiah 1 and answer the following questions:

- God spoke of knowing Jeremiah before he was born. Describe what this means.

- What were the words God placed in Jeremiah's mouth, and what are the words God has placed in your mouth? Give specific examples.

DAY 2
Read Jeremiah 2 and answer the following questions:

- How was it possible for Israel to turn away from the Lord?

- List some of the destructive teachings of our day.

DAY 3
Read Jeremiah 3 and answer the following questions:

- How does God use marriage and divorce as an illustration of His relationship with Israel?

- What would God do for Israel if she repented? Does this promise also to apply to our day? Explain.

DAY 4

Read Jeremiah 4 and answer the following questions:

- What does it mean to break up your fallow ground, and how hard is this to accomplish and why?

- What was the significance of the trumpet blowing? Are you and I expecting a trumpet to blow from heaven?

DAY 5

Read Jeremiah 5 and answer the following questions:

- How many righteous people were there in the city of Jerusalem? How many are in our city today?

- What role did the false prophets play in the downfall of God's people? Explain.

STUDY 21

Character Flaws
Focal Text: Numbers 23-24

Once again we find ourselves engaged in a behind-the-scenes look at God's work being accomplished through a pagan prophet by the name of Balaam. Look back at last week's study for background information.

Balaam's desires were pulled in different directions. He had been summoned by the king of the Moabites, King Balak, to come and pronounce a curse on Israel. At the same time he had been summoned by the true and living God to do just the opposite.

Yes, it is true: God uses all kinds of people to accomplish His will. In Balaam's case he finds himself between a rock and a hard place. He wants the payoff for carrying out King Balak's wishes, but at the same time he is afraid of offending the one true God. Balaam is riding the proverbial fence.

Jesus has taught us clearly never to ride the fence! In Mark 9:38–39 we are challenged to stand either for or against Jesus. In Mark 8:34–35 we are challenged to deny ourselves and take up our crosses and follow Him.

Balaam could not bring himself to be all-in either way; he must have concluded that he needed to leave his options open. We see such character flaws consistently in our day.

We see it in the world of sports. A franchise will give a young athlete a chance to make good. But when the player becomes accomplished, he or she leaves the team for a better deal. We see this in the halls of Congress as elected officials ride the fence between the views of special-interest groups and the will of the people who voted them into office. We see this in the lives of many believers who struggle with loyalty to God versus loyalty to the world.

What will Balaam decide, and what will each who read this decide? Be assured that whether Balaam decides for God or not, God will accomplish His will.

In these two chapters, no less than four times Balaam tries to ride the fence, but God keeps him from his plans. Out of these four attempts we find five character-building truths for our lives:

1. Sacrifice will not bring about a change in God's mind (Numbers 23:1–12).

King Balak meets Balaam and finds out why things are not working out as he thought. The king hears the dilemma and together these men decide to sacrifice to God in hopes that God would change His mind. They were to discover that God's plans are sealed in the heavens (Romans 11:29).

God's people were blessed, and God's people would be blessed (Genesis 13:6; 28:14). They would be as numerous as the sand of the sea.

2. God does not change (23:13–24).

This is so amazing in a world where people's character is swayed over and over in a period of time. Balaam declares God to be a God who never changes (23: 19). He is truth, and He has no need ever to change His mind. But we say God did change His mind on several occasions. The truth is that God relented when men repented.

James 1:17 reminds us of the true God of heaven who possesses sinless character. He is the God who has total clarity. He will never need to change His mind. This is a God we can trust. This God keeps His word.

Balaam is discovering that it is useless to attempt to change God's mind. You cannot stop God's will, change His will, or hold back His will. No change here.

3. You cannot be neutral concerning God's will (vv. 25–30).

Balak attempts to get Balaam to just be quiet. He is to say nothing. He is to let things play out. This must never be our viewpoint in this life. We must speak the words of God.

We must vote the words of God. We must live out the words of God.

4. God uses even pagan people to accomplish His will (Numbers 24).

As we turn the page to chapter 24, we read of God overshadowing Balaam's mind. Suddenly this pagan man is speaking the truth given to him by God.

Balaam declares that God will give victory to His people. It is not that God's people are perfect. They are simply blessed. Gane writes, "The imperfections of the Israelites were between them and God. While he disciplined them within their corporate boundaries, He did not air their dirty laundry in front of people from other nations. His firm resolve is to bless them" (Gane, 705).

Balaam also declares that God will favor those who favor Israel, and He will destroy those who are against His people. Even though Balaam's heart was not in blessing Israel, he had to submit to doing the Lord's will.

Balaam declares good news for God's people: God is sending a star who would conquer Israel's enemies. This is a dual prophecy. It speaks to the star of David and his coming to be king (2 Samuel 8:2–14) and also to another star who was to come (Revelation 22:16).

5. God did send one without flaws. His name is Jesus. He is coming again.

When Balaam declared that a star was coming, he had no clue that this would be the Messiah. But the star would indeed come (Colossians 2:15; Revelation 20:10, 14). This is the one we are to follow.

Brothers and sisters, God uses flawed people. This is good news. Without this we would not be usable by God. However, now that we follow Christ, we are to seek to be less flawless every day in our pursuit of accomplishing His will in this world, which includes godly character.

Balaam would go down in history as a man without godly character. His life would be swept away while he was still between two viewpoints riding the fence that eventually became his demise.

This week I want to challenge you to a life that has character—character that follows the principles set for us by the God who saved us.

ASSIGNMENTS FOR THE WEEK

DAY 1
Read Jeremiah 6 and answer the following questions:

- How does it make you feel when you read in verse 4, "Woe to us, for the day declines, for the shadows of evening lengthen"? How does this statement relate to where America finds herself today?

- How does character either aid or hinder God's refining process in the Christian's life?

DAY 2
Read Jeremiah 7 and answer the following questions:

- If you had been in the temple when Jeremiah spoke (vv. 1–4), how would you have responded? Explain.

- What character flaws was God pointing out in verses 4–10? Make a confession list of any character flaws in your own life.

DAY 3
Read Jeremiah 8 and answer the following questions:

- The character of Israel led to her demise. How difficult would it be to live with regret for sin? Notice verse 3 as you search for your answer.

- Is it difficult to live among people with serious character flaws? Explain.

DAY 4

Read Jeremiah 9 and answer the following questions:

- What does it mean to grieve for others?

- How would you respond to this question: Why has America lost her moral compass?

DAY 5

Read Jeremiah 10 and answer the following questions:

- What are the current ways of our nation? Consider verses 1–5 in your answer.

- How would the proper understanding of God change one's character?

STUDY 22

How Did We End Up Here?
Focal Text: Numbers 25

As the couple sat in the hospital waiting room, there was only one question on their minds: "How did we end up here?" Their child had been transported by ambulance to the hospital having barely survived a car accident that had been caused by his drug use. The parents had days to consider the why of this crisis. As they looked back, only one word came to mind: *compromise.*

It was author Alfred Adler who wrote the following: "It's easier to fight for one's principles than to live up to them" (cited in Gane, 717).

This couple had said they believed in living a drug-free life, but secretly they had been living the opposite. What they did occasionally was now holding their son's life for ransom. This week's devotional focuses on the reality of the downward spiral of compromise.

The nation of Israel was in the valley of Shittim. Just across the Jordon River lay the vicious people in the city of Jericho. God's people were waiting for the next move to be given to them by God. All systems were a go, God was with them (Psalm 91:9), and He was working for them. (We only have to remember God's power over the plans of Balak and Balaam in chapters 22–24).

The enemy's plans had been averted, but now he comes against God's people with another tactic called "compromise."

As the nation rested and reflected, there came into the camp a group of Moabite prostitutes. Yes, it is true—upon the advice of the false prophet Balaam, the king of Moab had sent these prostitutes to Israel.

Surely the people of God would send them back. Shockingly, the opposite takes place. The Bible records these words: "The men began to . . ." Suddenly we see God's people taking up the practices of compromise.

Question: What has happened to God's people?

Numbers 31:16 says that they heeded Balaam's counsel. Please tell me it is not so! I cannot believe the people of God would receive counsel from a false prophet. As I sit here in shock, I am reminded of the following:

- Many nations never seek the counsel of God (Deuteronomy 32:28).

- Many people never seek the counsel of God (Joshua 9:14).

- Many Christians fall into the trap of seeking counsel from the world (Proverbs 15:22; 20:18).

Christians must have a desire to live their lives according to the counsel of His will (Ephesians 1:11). Moses was there with Israel, but they did not seek his counsel. The Bible says in Isaiah 9:6 that the Messiah is "Wonderful Counselor," "Mighty God," but many never seek His counsel in the most crucial moments of life.

In this downward spiral the wicked counsel of Balaam led the people to take three downward steps:

1. Many of the people *leaned* into the fleshly trap of immoral actions.

2. Many of the people *fell* into the trap of idolatry.

3. Many of the people became *hooked* on the worship of a false god.

Such is the path of those who seek and follow the path of wicked counsel (2 Peter 2:3–10).

I am reminded of the story of a recovering alcoholic who sought the counsel of another recovering alcoholic who was riding in the car with him. As they came to an old familiar liquor store, he asked his friend, "Should we stop?" You finish the story.

The people of Israel sought the wisdom of a false prophet. The results were stinging, and they were devastating. God's righteous anger began striking the people with a plague. There would be 24,000 people who would die in the plague.

The path of compromise for the Christian always takes a person farther than he or she intends to go. Often the path of leaning, as was the case of the parents of the son in the hospital, leads to the open rebellion of the generations that come behind.

We see this in verse 6 as an Israelite man by the name of Zimri came before the weeping congregation with a cult prostitute. This man had no shame and no sorrow. What would be next for the people of Israel if this were allowed to continue?

The Bible says there was a priest by the name of Phinehas who was zealous for the Lord and His holiness. He took drastic action to remove the sin from the camp. The people had consecrated themselves to the thing of shame (Hosea 9:10).

Today more than ever the church needs to see the results of compromise. The church is facing its most crucial hour as there are many who are openly compromising the Word of God and the holiness of God (Revelation 2:14).

Only the zeal of one man turned the tide for Israel. The plague stopped. The question must be asked: Who will be zealous for the Lord in our day?

As the parents of the young man who was fighting for his life sat in the waiting room, they asked God this question: What should we do, Lord? In their spirits it was clear: they needed to repent of their compromise, and they needed to reestablish the lordship of Christ in their lives.

Brothers and sisters, as you and I consider the weight of this week's devotion, may we ask the following things of the Lord:

- Please show me any areas of comprise in my life.
- Teach me how to stand firm in a world gone crazy.
- Show me how to be bold and humble before a lost world.

ASSIGNMENTS FOR THE WEEK

Day 1
Read Jeremiah 11–12 and answer the following questions:

- Why is it so important to always listen to the counsel of God?

- If God disciplines His people for compromise, then explain why He does not seem to judge the wicked for their compromises.

Day 2
Read Jeremiah 13–14 and answer the following questions:

- Explain the significance of the loincloth in chapter 13.

- Had the people gone too far with God? If so, give reasons why.

Day 3
Read Jeremiah 15 and answer the following questions:

- Is it possible for one person to lead in turning a nation back to God? Give your answer in light of verse 1.

- Explain Jeremiah's complaints in this chapter and relate them to your own struggles in this day.

Day 4

Read Jeremiah 16–17 and answer the following questions:

- Was Jeremiah alone in the world in not having a wife? Give reasons for your answer.

- How does a person's or a nation's heart become so hard that they totally reject the counsel of God?

Day 5

Read Jeremiah 18 and answer the following questions:

- Explain how God can take a broken vessel and make it into a brand-new vessel. Give examples from your own life.

- Why do believers sometimes want to plot their own course in life? How does God bring such people back to the correct path?

STUDY 23

Getting a Second Chance
Focal Text: Numbers 26

Chapter 26 in the book of Numbers begins with a simple statement: "After the plague . . ." This statement helps the reader know that the events about to be related follow the events of chapter 25. But there is also another reason for this simple statement. It is a profound reason. Moses is cluing us in to this fact: God's people are getting a second chance.

Question: Are there any past decisions you would love to go back to so that you could make different decisions? I can honestly say yes. In my life there are some major things I would do differently, particularly from my teenage years.

God's people had made a terrible decision thirty-eight years earlier (Numbers 13–14). The majority voted to say no to God's will for their lives. The nation's view of God was low ("He can't do it"), and their view of their lives was even lower ("We can't do it").

Because of their decision the nation would spend the next forty years in the wilderness as the plague of God's judgment would weed out all those men who were twenty years old and above. So 603,577 men (1:46), have died. Only Moses, Joshua, and Caleb are still alive.

When the plague was finished (chapter 25), the judgment of this generation was complete. It was now a new day. The truth is—you and I do not get to have do-overs on our past. God forgives, and He charts a future for us. But the past days are in the rearview mirror of life.

God is giving Israel a second chance. The question is—What did the first generation teach the second generation? The book of Joshua gives us the answer to this question.

For our devotion I want to focus on what this scene in Numbers 26 actually teaches us about our lives and the responsibility we have to those who come after us. Every day other people are counting on us to be successful on the field of life.

You and I could never go back and erase the past, but we can affect the future if we follow time-tested truth. At this point Moses is directed to take a second census of the people. The number is about two thousand less (v. 51) than it had been thirty-eight years earlier.

The tribe of Simeon (vv. 12–14) has taken the greatest hit. Sproul comments, "Most likely this happened because of the constant rebellious heart of this tribe" (R. C. Sproul, *The*

Reformation Study Bible [Lake Mary, Fla.: Ligonier Ministries, 2005], 236).

On this day a new generation was being called to be courageous in following God's plan for their nation. I wonder how many of these young men were spiritually prepared by the wise counsel of their parents, grandparents, other close relatives, or friends.

This brings up an excellent point. Unless you and I are honest about our past, the next generation will make the same mistakes we made. Gane offers this helpful observation: "The second generation is back to the same situation as at the time of the first census, after losing nearly four decades" (Gane, 736). The plague was over, but was the rebellion over?

As I look at my own life, I know I have been forgiven from my past. But I fear I have passed on to my children my sinful nature. Maybe you feel this same way or maybe you are wondering, *What have my parents* (whether in the picture of your life or not) *passed on to me?*

Here are two Bible truths that will help us in this moment. These truths hit close to home in my life.

1. My rebellious spirit has cost me great loss in life.

Please take to heart what you have just read. There are moments when I feel shame. There are moments when I think, "I could have been so much more effective for the kingdom if I had not allowed my rebellious spirit [my flesh] to rule the day."

Maybe you are seeing the same rebellious spirit in your children. Have you been honest with them? Are you willing to speak God's truth into their hearts? Paul challenges us in Ephesians 4:25 to "speak the truth with his neighbor, for we are members one of another." If we do not speak the truth, the next generation will make the same mistakes we have made.

I am not suggesting that you open old wounds, nor am I suggesting that you share every detail of past rebellion. But I am suggesting that you get honest about the sinful DNA you have passed down to others. The Bible is clear that we should be "Redeeming the time, because the days are evil" (Ephesians 5:15 KJV).

2. My redeemed spirit has yielded me great success in life.

Every success in my life is God's success and not my own. The Lord Jesus Christ redeemed me from my old nature by giving me a new nature (2 Corinthians 5:17). The Lord Jesus Christ empowered me to overcome the rebellious spirit within me (1 John 5:4–5).

As I write this chapter, tears are flowing down my cheeks as I realize how much of my family's past failures have been broken in my life. The chains and curses in my family tree have been stopped cold in their path by the power of the cross. God can do the same in your life!

This new generation stood in a new place. Moses will give them wisdom for the future by sharing the truth about their past. We see this wisdom in the book of Deuteronomy. This new generation would do what the first could not and did not do.

Brothers and sisters, our second chance often comes through those who come behind us. Years earlier in Numbers 14 the people used their fear of their children being murdered by the enemy as an excuse for not obeying the Lord (14:31–32), but now God will use these children, who have become adults, to accomplish greatness.

It is my prayer that the generations who come by us and behind us will accomplish the will of the Lord. I leave you with the words of Paul in Ephesians 5:17: "Do not be foolish but understand what the will of the Lord is."

ASSIGNMENTS FOR THE WEEK

DAY 1
Read Jeremiah 19–20 and answer the following questions:

- Jeremiah uses the example of a broken flask to illustrate the brokenness coming to God's people. What illustration can you give to help people around you understand the brokenness that comes with rebellion?

- Jeremiah is persecuted for his faith. Why do you and I fear to tell the truth about our past and fear to tell others about our faith? Explain.

DAY 2
Read Jeremiah 21–24 and answer the following questions:

- What moral failures do we see in our nation today?

- How does the promise of the "righteous Branch" in chapter 23 give us hope in a morally failing world?

DAY 3
Read Jeremiah 25–29 and answer the following questions:

- Why was God allowing judgment to come? See 25:8. What guilt do you and I have if we fail to give people God's Word?

- How do we direct our children to truth when many of their friends are telling them about a different path?

DAY 4
Read Jeremiah 30–33 and answer the following questions:

- How long does a person have to feel the weight of his or her rebellion before he or she repents? Is it hard to wait for this day with someone you love?

- Do you believe God can turn mourning into joy? Why?

DAY 5
Read Jeremiah 34–36 and answer the following questions:

- What are the dreams you have for your family? Write them down.

- Have you shared those dreams with your family? Call them this week.

STUDY 24

Facing Your Failures
Focal Text: Numbers 27:12-23

As I look back over my life, I have so many awesome memories from my childhood. My mother often spoke of my childhood as being spotless. Oh, the love of a mother! Anyone who knew me knew better than to believe I was spotless. I carry with me to this day the scars of failures. I can still remember my mother on rare occasions deciding to delay punishment for my sin until my dad got home from work. She would say, "Let's wait to see what you dad has to say."

My day would usually be destroyed because the cloud of the coming judgment was ever before me. I would prepare myself by coming up with great excuses, or I would come up with easy suggestions for my punishment. But it was always the same: when I saw Dad I melted and accepted what he decided. Even in those early days God was teaching me to face my failures.

As we come to Numbers 27, Moses writes about what some might say was a difficult and unfair moment. But nothing could be farther from the truth. Moses teaches us how to face our failures, and in doing so he points us to both a path beyond our failures and to the one person who gives us freedom from our failures.

First let's focus on the path beyond our failures.

Moses has spent over forty years with God's sheep. He began with a miracle meeting with God in which God called him to lead His people out of over four hundred years of bondage (Exodus 3). God was with Moses. God worked miracle after miracle in leading the people out. Moses led the people to Mt. Sinai, where he received the Ten Commandments. From there it was supposed to be on to the promised land. You know how the people caved in with open rebellion (Numbers 13–14). The next forty years would be filled with difficulty. However, Moses led as a faithful shepherd.

But there was that one day, a day of Moses's personally caving in. We remember it so vividly in Numbers 20. Moses decided that for this one hour he was going to choose to do things in his own way. James 4:17 says, "So whoever knows the right thing to do and fails to do it, for him it is sin." Moses had failed to honor God before His people. The judgment of God was swift and serious.

The Lord reminded Moses of this in our focal text. Question: What would Moses do? Moses had chosen the path of facing his failures in a way that moved him beyond the failures.

- **Moses accepted God's decision.**

Read those words again. Moses did not question God, doubt God, or resist God's decision. He knew God was just, righteous, and holy. He also knew God was a God of great grace.

Moses understood that the treason in his heart had been real in that moment. He knew God was showing the people how serious rebellion really was. Without a doubt, Moses was grieved by his own sin, and clearly he did not want to live in it. I believe he modeled James 4:7–10 in his heart's response.

- **Moses obeyed God's directions.**

The Lord speaks to Moses about what is in his future (Numbers 27:12–13). In the days ahead after praying a prayer of blessing on God's people (Deuteronomy 33), Moses would be led by God up a hill where he would see into the promised land (Deuteronomy 34:1–4). Can you see him there (Deuteronomy 32:49)? I see Moses standing on his tiptoes holding his staff to keep him from tipping over. I see him straining with his eyes to see every bit of the land he can see. I can almost see tears falling onto his beard.

Do you see him with hands raised high praising God for what is to come? He knows God is keeping His promise. Moses's family and nation will live in freedom in that place.

This last journey would not be of a broken man but of a blessed man.

Brothers and sisters, you and I are called to accept God's decision and obey His directions. God has much for you and me beyond our failures. Check out 1 John 1:5–10. We will never get beyond our failures until we face them as God prescribes for us.

- **Moses cared about what God cares about.**

Instead of engaging in self-pity as many others would have done, Moses expresses his concern that his people would have a good leader to replace him.

Moses cried out, "Lord they need the man you choose to lead them." Moses understood the omniscience of God. God knows everything about everyone. He knew who would faithfully shepherd the people after Moses was gone.

Oh, the joy that must have filled Moses heart as God said, "Joshua, step forward." Moses had mentored Joshua for over forty years. Together they had battled, sought God's will, stood before Him, and stood with God even against the entire nation.

As I read these words, again tears fill my eyes as I realize how much Moses models for me how a faithful shepherd is to lead—he cares for what God cares about. Gane observes, "Had Moses not possessed a character of granite, and at the same time a gentle humility surpassing that of all others (Numbers 12:3), history would have been a lot different" (Gane, 744).

You and I might be tempted to say, "That was Moses—I can't be like Moses." This is true, but God never says He wants us to be like Moses.

Second, let's focus on the one person who can lead us beyond our failures.

This one person is Jesus Christ. "Like Moses, Jesus offered to give up everything for his people. But He went beyond Moses, becoming a 'lamb' and dying for us (John 1:29; 1 Corinthians 5:7)" (Gane, 745).

Jesus has come to be our Great Shepherd. All who come to Him find His sacrifice sufficient for their failures. All find him to be kind, forgiving, and a shepherd who will lead them beyond their failures. Who would not want to follow such a leader?

Isn't it time for you to face your failures before the Great Shepherd?

ASSIGNMENTS FOR THE WEEK

DAY 1
Read Jeremiah 37–38 and answer the following questions:

- What are the most difficult tasks of leadership in the twenty-first century?

- How would you have responded if you were treated as Jeremiah was?

DAY 2
Read Jeremiah 39–40 and answer the following questions:

- Who loses the most when leaders fail to lead? Explain.

- Why did God choose to favor Jeremiah in this time? Does God still favor His leaders in hard times?

DAY 3
Read Jeremiah 41–43 and answer the following questions:

- How difficult would it be to lead a people who do not really intend to follow?

- Explain how to lead a family to obey God in times of difficulty.

DAY 4

Read Jeremiah 44–51 and answer the following questions:

- Why was God judging all these nations?

- What does this all mean for our nation?

DAY 5

Read Jeremiah 52 and answer the following questions:

- It was heartbreaking to see all these things. What would be the worst thing that could happen to our nation?

- Explain how you want to make a difference in our world.

STUDY 25

Making Your Calendar Count
Focal Text: Numbers 28–29

Each year it seems that I find myself more and more pressed for time in my daily activities. Could it be possible that my calendar is controlling my life? As I write this devotion, I am looking at my calendar for the holiday season. Here is my honest reflection: I wonder how much on my calendar will really count for eternity. I often meet people who confess that they are extremely busy when I ask them how they are doing.

Kevin DeYoung wrote a book a few years ago titled *Crazy Busy* (Wheaton, Ill.: Crossway, 2013). Here are two quotes from the book:

- Busyness kills more Christians than bullets. (32)

- Busyness is like sin: kill it, or it will be killing you. (30)

As I took the time to read through the chapters in our focal text, I became very aware of God's clear reasoning for giving the nation a yearly calendar.

Before this time in Israel's life "calendars were not very important to the Jewish people. They worked from sunup to sundown, counting the months by the phases of the moon. They watched the seasons come and go. God had promised them 'seedtime and harvest, cold and heat, summer and winter, day and night,' and they were content. Each day was a sacred gift from God" (Warren W. Wiersbe, *The Wiersbe Bible Commentary: The Complete Old Testament in One Volume* [Colorado Springs: David C. Cook, 2007], 235).

However, things were changing. The foreign land they were about to enter would push the people to limits they had never encountered before. The nations who presently occupied the promised land had their own gods and their own daily events that fueled their worship of false gods. Israel needed to have a calendar that would lead them to live their lives for the one true God.

The chapters before us taught the people about the importance of each day on the calendar, each weekend on the calendar, and special days on the calendar that always directed them to remember who they were worshiping and who they were working for and with.

I want to challenge you to take time to read about all the special days as well as the Sabbath day. Each of these days point us to understand how great Jesus is in His fulfilling everything the special days stood for. Let me give you just a sample:

The Day of Atonement (29:7–11)

Today we refer to this day as Yom Kippur. This day was on the calendar once each year. The people were to celebrate it in the seventh month of their calendar year (October). The month begins with the blowing of trumpets signifying a new year, Rosh Hashanah (Leviticus 23:23–25). Ten days later would be the Day of Atonement.

On the Day of Atonement, the most sacred day, the most sacred priest would enter the most sacred place to make atonement. The high priest would carry a payment for the sins of the people. The people during the past year had sinned, some more than others, but all had sinned (Romans 3:23). On this day the priest would come before the Lord to make a payment for all their wrongs.

The people would come to this day with repentant hearts, confessing their sins. They would mourn for their sin (1 John 1:9). They would reflect on who God was: "Our Father which art in heaven, Hallowed be thy name" (Matthew 6:9 KJV). This was a day when they felt the joy of forgiveness. All their sins were being washed away! (Psalm 103:12).

But on this day they were also reminded of what God was going to do in sending a Savior. This Savior would come to do more than cover their sin. He would come to take away their sin. Hebrews 9:11–12 says it best:

> But when Christ appeared as a high priest of the good things that have come, then through the greater and more perfect tent (not made with hands, that is, not of this creation) he entered once for all into the holy places, not by means of the blood of goats and calves but by means of his own blood, thus securing an eternal redemption.

When Christ died on the cross He became the eternal atonement for all who come to Him as their Lord and Savior. Each week the church now gathers on the first day of the week to celebrate what Jesus did for us, to celebrate the cleansing power of God's Son (1 John 1:7).

The nation of Israel would find God's calendar to be their strength in a foreign land. But there would come the day when foreign gods would lead them away from devotion to God. The people would still observe the days, but it would be only an observance. This should be a strong reminder for us never to allow God's day to be replaced on our calendars.

Surely you know the value in the days God has given us. Here are two calendar truths for us:

1. God wants every person to put Him first in each day of his or her life.

God is more concerned about our worship than He is our work. He is far more interested in our fellowship with Him than our feats of accomplishment that honor us as much as they honor Him.

This is why God wants all people to put on their daily calendar: time with Him. When we begin the day in worship and fellowship, we are reminded of what each day is about. We are able to redeem our time in the world. Our calendars become our mission fields (Ephesians 5:16).

2. God wants us to set aside one day each week to gather with others for worship.

We call this day Sunday. On this day we are reminded of who God is and what He calls us to do each day. On this day we are giving testimony to the world of our dependence on God for our every need. On this day we are refueled, and we are refreshed as we rest from the weekly calendar. A calendar so filled with life apart from God covers up "the rot in a person's soul" (DeYoung, 31). All people need the cleansing that comes from the worship and Word given each week. It is directed to our souls.

God taught His people to follow His calendar. When the people obeyed, they made the calendar of their lives count. The question now becomes "What about our calendars?"

ASSIGNMENTS FOR THE WEEK

DAY 1
Read Hebrews 1 and answer the following questions:

- According to the writer of Hebrews 1, who is Jesus?

- What is the significance of Jesus "sitting down at the right hand of God"?

DAY 2
Read Hebrews 2 and answer the following questions:

- Explain why believers drift away from God, and tell how we can keep ourselves from drifting.

- How does Jesus bring many sons to glory?

DAY 3
Read Hebrews 3–4 and answer the following questions:

- Orthodox Jews still hold Moses as being greater than Jesus. Why do we worship Jesus and not Moses? Explain.

DAY 4
Read Hebrews 5 and answer the following questions:

- Why did God appoint Jesus to be our high priest?

- Who was Melchizedek?

DAY 5

Read Hebrews 6–7 and answer the following questions:

- How is it possible for someone to know about God and still turn away?

- What does the writer mean when he writes, "He always lives to make intercession for them" (6:25)? Explain.

STUDY 26

The Wall of Broken Vows
Focal Text: Numbers 30

I can still remember her question to her husband. Her words were direct, and they flowed from a heart that was broken. Her husband had just admitted to a three-year affair. (Some details have been changed to protect the people involved). This broken woman asked, "Did our vows mean nothing to you? I guess twenty-eight years of marriage counted for nothing."

Twenty-eight years earlier this young couple, filled with love, stood before a pastor both believing they wanted God to be over their marriage. Theologically speaking, they believed God was the tie that would bind them together forever (Ecclesiastes 4:9–10). But now, all these years later, this couple had hit the wall of reality. The husband had built a wall of broken vows that stood between him and his wife of twenty-eight years.

For many who read this, the reality of this story hits too close to home. It is the biggest wall in your life. You want to go from bondage to blessing, but you do not know how. Still for others, you are trying to figure out the vows you have made in a desperate moment in your past or maybe even now. You said to God, "If you will get me out of this, I will . . ." Now you are standing face to face with the payday of your vow. Gane offers insight into our souls here: "The problem with promises (vows) is that they are easy to make—especially in the heat of the moment when there is need to express caring, gratitude, or a desire for reconciliation—but can be more difficult to fulfill than first imagined" (Gane, 763).

This week's focal text leads us to consider the subject of vows. In context, God's directions are unique toward His covenant family. However, they lead us to investigate vows in a biblical way.

A vow is a voluntary promise that was, and is, supposed to be kept if the vow was made right before God. Vows usually were either for times of devotion or times of abstaining. Occasionally they were offered in bargaining with God to destroy others. One of the most familiar examples of someone who made a vow is that of Hannah, described in 1 Samuel 1:11. Her vow was right before God. We see in the example of Jacob a common vow: "God, I will serve you if you . . ." (Genesis 28:18–22).

In our focal text, Numbers 30, God is specifically speaking of vows given by people whose circumstances changed after giving a vow. Such people could not possibly know what the future held. We see an example of a single woman who made a vow before she was married (30:6–8). But now that she was married, her husband did not agree with the vow. In this case she could be absolved from the vow. But in all other cases, except what was outlined here, vows were to be kept before God.

Why did God take this so seriously? First, the vow was offered voluntarily. God expects us to be a people of our word (Ecclesiastes 5:1–4). Jesus strongly condemned the abuse of vows (Matthew 15:4–6). Second, breaking a vow meant something had happened in the person's life with his or her character, or a grievous sin had taken place.

Question: Have you ever made a vow? If you answered yes, then you know how hard it is to keep it. Vows are amazing things before God if we approach them and keep them in the correct ways.

I want to give you five biblically directed suggestions concerning vows:

1. Make sure you are right with God before you consider making a vow (Psalm 116:18).

2. Make sure you are vowing for the right reasons (1 Corinthians 10:31).

3. Make sure you consider the amount of sacrifice that is needed in making your vow (Luke 14:28–30).

4. Make sure you are committed to the one you are making a vow before (Deuteronomy 28:23).

5. Make sure you put in place healthy reminders of the vows you have made (Ecclesiastes 5:4).

Now before we end this week's devotion, I want to speak to those who have blown it with vows. I think about the brokenness of the man who had shattered his wedding vows. He genuinely wanted to know how to be forgiven and restored. Here is what the Bible says:

1. Seek God's forgiveness (1 John 1:9).

2. Seek the forgiveness of the one you have shattered in breaking your vow (1 John 1:5–8).

3. Commit to earning back the trust of the ones you have shattered (Psalm 15:4).

Still others who are reading this are saying, "What about me? I am the victim here." If this is true of you, I am so sorry for what you have endured. But be assured that God has a future for you. Here are three reminders for you:

1. God is trustworthy. He never breaks a vow. Look to Him (Revelation 22:5–6).

2. People are sinners. On our best days we fail each other. This is no excuse, but it reminds us of our need to give grace to others.

204

3. Stay on top of your relationships. Be accountable and demand accountability from those who enter into vows with you.

I am happy to say that the wife and husband found sweet grace and mercy in their marriage. She forgave him as he showed his repentance and his desire to live a redeemed life. It was a long journey, but it was made because the wife refused to allow his breaking the vow to lead to her breaking the vow. May the Lord use the truth of vows to help you scale the wall of reality.

ASSIGNMENTS FOR THE WEEK

DAY 1

Read Hebrews 8–9 and answer the following questions:

- In what ways can our high priest (Christ) help us to make decisions in difficult moments?

- What role does our making vows to God play in our efforts to "serve the living God" (9:14)? Does God require us to make vows? Explain.

DAY 2

Read Hebrews 10 and answer the following questions:

- What if any vow did Jesus make to God the Father in connection to coming to this world?

- How does our attendance at church help us in our walk with the Lord? Explain.

DAY 3

Read Hebrews 11 and answer the following questions:

- What vows did Abraham make to God?

- Did Gideon make vows, or did he ask questions? Explain the difference.

DAY 4

Read Hebrews 12 and answer the following questions:

- How does Jesus's sacrifice for us lead us to a place of complete trust in Him?

- What role does God's discipline play in our making of vows?

DAY 5

Read Hebrews 13 and answer the following questions:

- Why were people being placed in prison in the time of Hebrews? Explain.

- Do you and I have to make vows in order to be effective as Christ-followers? Explain.

———◆———

STUDY 27

Holy War
Focal Text: Numbers 31

The day was December 7. The year was 1941. The naval base at Pearl Harbor, Hawaii, was just coming to life when it happened. The Japanese Imperial Navy had launched planes from their carriers earlier that morning and were now coming into Hawaii as the sun rose. Suddenly and without warning they attacked. Before the battle was over, 2,400 Americans had been killed and another 1,200 wounded.

This unprovoked attack on our nation led the United States fully into World War II. By the time the war was over, 400,000 lives had been lost. Such is the result of humanity's attempt to destroy each other.

Question: Is there ever a time when men are justified in going to war? An even deeper question would be this: Does God ever sanction holy war?

These are very timely questions as we approach the last assignment of Moses before his death. These are needed questions as we read of God's directions to Israel to engage in "holy war." You read the last sentence correctly—God directs His people into holy war. The ESV identifies this war as "the Lord's vengeance" (v. 3).

In this moment reality has come to place a wall in front of our teaching about our God. The Bible clearly teaches of the mercy and kindness of God. John 3:16 stands as God's greatest word concerning His love for all humanity. The Bible also teaches us of the kindness and patience of God. According to Romans 2:4, He is a God who is rich in kindness and patience.

If these things be true, how can we justify the actions directed by God in Numbers 31? The wall of reality is raised higher when we read such statements as this: "Those of us who accept the entire Bible as the Word of God have no choice but to admit that God sometimes gives up on groups of people and chooses to destroy them" (Gane, 772).

Brothers and sisters, I honestly struggle with the author's use of the words "God sometimes gives up." Our task as always is to seek our answers in God's Word. The journey from bondage to blessing must begin and end in God's Word.

So let us first look at the content of this chapter. The Lord commands Moses to lead the people into war (v. 7) with the people of Midian. God instructs His army to kill every man and to kill the women who participated in leading Israel into idolatry (Numbers 25). The army carries out the orders in killing all the men, but they leave the women alive.

When Moses comes to the battle, he sees the women left alive. He calls for the killing of only the women who were part of the sinful trap of God's people. Once the battle is over, it is a miracle for God's people—not one person in God's army has been hurt (31:49).

It would be easy in this moment to raise the patriotic flag and rejoice in the victory. But we still have the questions before us. Does God sanction holy war, and are men ever justified in going to war?

Let me answer the second question first. I believe the Scripture is clear that God does ordain war when it comes to the defense of our lives and in rescuing the lives of others (Romans 13:1–2).

It is to the first question that people struggle with. Iain Duguid gives us amazing insight here: "This conflict between Israel and Midian is no ordinary human war. Nor is it an act of ethnic cleansing on Israel's part. There is in fact nothing ethnic about this conflict, for this war is part of God's larger war on sin and evil" (cited in Gane, 330).

God is directing His people into a unique war that removed Israel's enemies out of the land that was to belong to His people. There are no fewer than five truths we need that lead us to understand God and holy war:

1. God judges all rebellion impartially. The God of Israel has already judged His people for their part in the sinful rebellion in chapter 25. Now it is time for the people of Midian to be judged for their sin (25:16–18).

2. God is a just God. He has been patient with the people of Midian in their rebellion. Gane writes, "God kept His people waiting in Egypt until the end of four centuries waiting for the people to repent, but they did not" (Gane, 773).

3. You and I are not God. As much as we want to be impartial in judgment, it is impossible. There is only one qualified to inflict vengeance. His name is Jesus (Romans 12:14–20; Hebrews 10:30; Revelation 16:7).

4. The church does not have a mandate from God ever to wage a holy war. "Our enemies aren't flesh and blood, and our weapons are spiritual" (Wiersbe, 297).

5. Someday all people will face God's final judgment (Revelation 20:11–14). It is not an earthly king we will stand before, and it is not an earthly judge. You and I will stand before the King of Kings and Lord of Lords.

On that dreaded day in 1941 the nation of Japan could not say they were justified in their war against our nation. On this day no human being can say he or she is justified in killing people because it is holy war. What our world needs is the love of God.

ASSIGNMENTS FOR THE WEEK

DAY 1
Read Zechariah 1 and answer the following questions:

- How does repentance lead us to victory in our spiritual wars?

- Why was God calling His people to look beyond their present circumstances? How can you and I find hope in difficult days?

DAY 2
Read Zechariah 2 and answer the following questions:

- If God protects His people, then why do we worry?

- Do you ever have moments with God when you feel His presence so strongly that you are silenced by it? Give an illustration.

DAY 3
Read Zechariah 3 and answer the following questions:

- How do we know when a leader is teaching a false gospel?

- Explain how God could remove the sin of a nation in a single day.

DAY 4

Read Zechariah 4 and answer the following questions:

- When God points out our weaknesses, how does it make us feel? Explain.
- How can God's power enable a person to accomplish the impossible?

DAY 5

Read Zechariah 5 and answer the following questions:

- Explain how God is both a loving God and a just God at the same time.
- Why can God not tolerate sin in His people?

STUDY 28

It's Bigger than Me
Focal Text: Numbers 32

My mother used to tell me, "Keith, you will love your grandchildren even more than you love your own children." Now that Sherry and I have a grandson, we love him passionately. One of the things little ones always do is to reach for everything in their sight because they believe everything has been placed before them for their taking.

As we grow to maturity, God intends for our thought processes to change. For instance, Paul writes the following in Philippians 2:4: "Let each of you look not only to his own interests, but also to the interests of others."

On our journey from bondage to blessing, we must deal with the reality of what we are born with. Yes, it is true that we are born with a heart bent on self. Self builds a large wall that tries to keep us from God's view of life being bigger than us.

We see this reality in Numbers 32. Moses had led God's people to victory over the Midianites (chapter 31). It is here where the tribes of Reuben, Gad, and the half-tribe of Manasseh make a decision. These tribes, more than the others, had been blessed with many livestock. To them this conquered land was the best place for them to tend their cattle and to raise their families.

The leaders of these tribes come to Moses and the elders of Israel. Here is their thought process: "If it pleases the leadership, extend grace to us and give us possession and ownership of this land." Brothers and sisters, if we are going to scale the wall of self, we need to consider two truths, and we need to make a lifetime decision.

The first truth is this: Often our first consideration in life is *ourselves.*

The Bible teaches us of God's love for His people in His unfailing provision for all their needs (Matthew 6:25–33). But how often do we forget this? When we forget this truth, we usually begin to focus on viewpoints such as "I need to take care of my family first"; "I need more than I have now"; and "I am only seeking what is fair." The half-brother of Jesus spoke clearly about this truth in James 4:1–4.

Moses had seen this type of attitude before, and he reminded these people of what it had cost the nation in the days of their parents. If these tribes decided to focus on their own interests, the rest of the tribes would become discouraged.

When I think about Christmas I am always reminded of the self-sacrificing love of Jesus in coming to this earth (Luke 1:30–33, 54–55; Luke 2:10–14; Philippians 2:8–9). He put our needs first. Second Corinthians 5:21 teaches us the love of Jesus in becoming sin for us so that we might receive His righteousness.

Moses understood that the other tribes would be frustrated, and if the "me first" viewpoint spread, there was sure destruction ahead. If they turned back, God would turn His back on them.

Everything Moses was saying was true. It is the same today. If you and I live with only our own lives in focus, others will be discouraged because we are called to be God's hands and feet to others. If we are not giving and investing in others' lives, they will become discouraged because they think God has forgotten or abandoned them. If we do not invest in others, our sin will eventually ruin our families and our churches.

The second truth is this: It is our faith that leads us to consider others.

Notice the refreshing response given by the tribes to Moses beginning in verse 16. The tribes commit to taking up arms with their brothers. They only ask for their families to be sheltered and their cattle to be cared for before they go.

Brothers and sisters, you and I are called by God to partner with others in the family of God (Philippians 1:5). The tribes commit to staying with the battle until it is completed. Before us is truly a faith that leads the people to care about where others are. This is the hope we have when faith is working in us.

Moses makes two promises: God will bless them to return to their inheritance if they are faithful to their brothers and sisters. But the opposite is also true: God will judge the people if they do not fulfill their commitment.

The tribes commit to being God's ministers for their brethren. How refreshing to see a people who will work the land and do battle for the purposes of the Lord! Moses must have smiled as the people made their commitment. God certainly smiled because He could see into the future. He knew these people would keep their commitments.

Brothers and sisters, all we have to do to see the outcome of their faith is to read the book of Joshua. In Joshua 22 we read the wonderful news. The people had kept their faith commitment. So many times in life Christians make commitments based on emotion only, and very soon they turn away from the commitment when the emotions wear off. But not these tribes. Their decision was one of genuine faith.

Brothers and sisters, you and I needed this chapter. We needed this reality checkup. It's now time for you and me to make the lifetime decision, if not already made, to live a life for others.

For those who embrace this decision, there are at least two blessings that come. First, there is a blessing of a life lived for others here on this earth. Second, there is an eternal life of blessings to come in heaven. Jesus said, "And everyone who has left houses or brothers or sisters or father or mother or children or lands, for my name's sake, will receive a hundredfold and will inherit eternal life. But many who are first will be last, and the last first" (Matthew 19:29–30).

I challenge all who read this chapter to decide to put God first. When you do, He will show you the bigger picture, and He will bless you for your decision.

ASSIGNMENTS FOR THE WEEK

DAY 1
Read Zechariah 6 and answer the following questions:

- Whose side are the chariots and horses on? Whose side are you on?

- What impact has God's branch had in the world and in your own personal life?

DAY 2
Read Zechariah 7 and answer the following questions:

- How does being a serving member of a church (6:15) help a person to grow in his or faith to help others?

- Why is obedience to God more crucial than sacrifice to God?

DAY 3
Read Zechariah 8 and answer the following questions:

- How can the truth of Christ's coming encourage you as you wait for God's help in a trying time?

- List some of the things you are waiting for from God.

DAY 4

Read Zechariah 9–11 and answer the following questions:

- When you think of God as a coming judge, how does this make you feel?

- What does it mean when God says that He is coming to avenge His people?

DAY 5

Read Zechariah 12–14 and answer the following questions:

- What will it look like in the world on God's day of judgment?

- How does the coming celebration encourage you in these days of difficulty?

STUDY 29

He's Coming
Focal Text: Numbers 33–34

It happens every Christmas when we get together with family. Maybe it's the same in your family. We gather together, and before long the stories of days gone by begin being told. Sometimes we share the details of an event, but at other times we just the mention of the event from the past causes all of us to laugh. The older I get the more I cherish those moments for what they mean. But at the same time I look forward between our times together to making more memories to come. The closer the time gets for family to visit, the more excited I become.

The Christmas season always does the same with me when it comes to my walk with Jesus. In this season I look back to Jesus's coming. He was and is the God who came to our world (our home). But at the same time I look forward to Jesus's second coming. He is the God who is coming to take His people to another world (His home).

As we open our Bibles to our focal text, it is with the reality of knowing that Israel has much history to consider and she has much history-making before her. In chapter 33 Moses lists forty-two stops in recounting Israel's previous forty years of history. Obviously these were recorded as reminders of God's faithfulness and goodness to His people, stirring us to thankfulness for His provision.

Could it be that you and I need to be stirred afresh to be thankful for what God has done for us? Could it be that many who read this need to hear for the first time of the goodness of God to humanity? I believe the answer to both questions is yes.

Let's take a fresh look at Israel's journeys with a viewpoint of discovering how this applies to us.

Moses writes, "These are the journeys . . ." (KJV).

First, we see the arrival of deliverance. God had announced to His people that He had come to deliver them (Exodus 6:1). Forty plus years later, Moses begins with the story of God's arrival to deliver. This deliverance happened on Passover. The last plague of God was unleashed upon Egypt (Exodus 12). Moses remembered the day of triumph as he described the Hebrews' exodus from Egypt. The Lord's hand was on them. God struck down the enemies of His people. He defeated the false gods by proving they were unable to protect their people from the one true God.

Do you see the people going out of the city as the people of Egypt were burying their firstborn sons? Brothers and sisters, do you see the imagery here? Almost two thousand years ago God informed the world of the arrival of His Son (Matthew 1:18–25; Luke 1:28–32). The Son of God would arrive, and He would die in our place (1 Timothy 2:4–6). Christmas reminds us of the arrival of the God who came to be with us (Luke 2:8–14).

Second, we see the advancement of the delivered. We read of forty-one more stops on the journey to the blessing. One author divided the chapter into the following headings: "The faithfulness of God; The forgiveness of God; and The future of God's people" (Gane, 348–49).

With each stage God was always faithful, and with each stage Israel was either faithful or she was unfaithful. In every unfaithful stop God had forgiven His people. Now the people stood ready to embrace their future.

Oh, how often we need to be reminded of these truths! Last evening as I slept I was suddenly awakened with the awareness of a burden in my heart. I thought, "I'm fifty-one years old. How much longer will I live?" My brother-in-law, Pastor Stanley Long, died recently at fifty-three, being in the prime of his ministry. I began getting anxious as I considered what is to come with my life. How will I finish? In the midst of my fear the Lord reminded me, "Keith, I will someday come for you and take you to where I live." God impressed upon me this truth: He is always completely in control.

Maybe you are reading this while in crisis. The crisis could be a physical problem. It could be the terror of trying to raise three children by yourself as you hold down a job. It could be not knowing how to get out of the bondage you are in.

Strengthen yourself in Jesus, knowing that just as with Moses, God will triumphantly bring out all who call upon His name (Romans 10:13).

Third, we see the assault on the enemy. Beginning in Numbers 33:50, the assault begins. God tells Israel to put her boots on the ground across the Jordan. Brothers and sisters, it is in this season that we remember Jesus's coming as our Emmanuel. He came and put His boots on the ground of this world. The forces of hell began to shake as they heard the news with the shepherds, "He has come!"

The assault was on. The people were to drive out the enemies of God. They were to destroy their idols. They were to demolish their places of worship. Brothers and sisters, you and I await a Savior who will come to remove all His enemies (Revelation 19).

Fourth, we see the accomplishments anticipated. When the assault was completed, the people would take possession of the land. They would dwell in the promised land.

Again I ask, "Do you see the imagery here?" All that Jesus accomplished for us on the cross will find its fulfillment in His second coming. Psalm 23:6 says, "I shall dwell in the house of the Lord forever." Oh, how wonderful the believer's inheritance in heaven will be (Ephesians 1:11, 14, 18; Colossians 3:24).

As you and I celebrate with God's people, we also must heed God's warning to them (v. 55). Along the journey we are called to walk in a way that honors the Lord. Unless we honor the Lord, there will be loss of rewards in heaven.

I must admit that not every memory I have of our family is good. I have often failed my family. But with honest confession there has always been forgiveness. Maybe this season is a time of failure for you. Look at what Jesus did for you, and consider how much He loves you in this moment of your life. Ask Him for forgiveness, and then celebrate what He has done for you. There is coming a day when Jesus will return to take His people to His home where there will be no failing moments. Oh, what a day that will be!

This week you will be challenged to be thankful for His first coming, and you will be challenged to be ready for His second coming.

ASSIGNMENTS FOR THE WEEK

Day 1
Read 1 Samuel 1–3 and answer the following questions:

- Why did Hannah so desperately want a child?

- How did God use her child in His plan?

Day 2
Read 1 Samuel 4–7 and answer the following questions:

- In what ways did Eli fail his sons and his people?

- How was Samuel's ministry different than Eli's?

Day 3
Read 1 Samuel 8–11 and answer the following questions:

- Why was Samuel's heart broken when God's people wanted a king?

- Why did the people want a king like Saul? Why do people like Jesus in a stable but do not want Him on the throne of their lives?

Day 4

- **Read 1 Samuel 12–16 and answer the following questions:**

  - Why was David a different type of king than Saul?

  - Why did God choose David to be king?

Day 5

Read 1 Samuel 17–20 and answer the following questions:

- Describe what truth we gain in David's story of killing Goliath.

- Jonathan and David had a kindred brotherhood seldom seen in this world. How does their friendship challenge you to be a better friend?

STUDY 30

A Home for Sinners
Focal Text: Numbers 35-36

A single mother began attending a local church every
other Sunday. Her husband had left her without
any resources and she was struggling to survive. She said,
"Something inside of me was whispering, 'You need God.'"
In her effort to find Him, she began attending the local
church. Little did she know that God was not in that church.
A few months in, the pastor asked to meet with her at the
end of the service. He was very nice but to the point. He
said, "Some of the ladies here are offended at your dress, and
they are offended that you are divorced. I am going to have
to ask you not to come back anymore." In shock, the single
mother poured out her heart with one simple question: Is
there anywhere a sinner can go?

The Bible teaches us about a place called heaven (John
14:3; Revelation 21–22). The spender of that place is beyond
human description.

The question for our devotion today is this: "Can sinners go to heaven?" In our theology we respond with yes. But in reality do we believe this is true?

In the strangest of places, Numbers 35, we find truth that helps us answer this question. You and I are at the end of our study in Numbers. When we began all those weeks ago, we joined Israel thirteen months into their journey from bondage to blessing. We have walked with Israel in the reality of a real world. Now Israel was ready to go in. Moses was following God's directions in completing Israel's directions for how the people were to live once they were firmly established in the blessing of the promised land.

As Moses completes God's directions, we read of two important divisions being made. The Levites had been given the tithe that came from the other tribes, so they were not given territory in the land. So now God gives them forty-eight cities. "They needed to live somewhere. God spread the cities throughout the land so there would be maintained religious unity in the nation" (Gane, 795).

In the designation of those forty-eight cities, God set aside six cities (three on each side of the Jordan River) designated as "cities of refuge." These cities were places where people who committed unintentional murder could flee for safety from their accusers. Warren Wiersbe gives us insight:

> The nation had no police force, and the el-
> ders in each city constituted a "court" to consider
> capital crimes. If a person accidentally killed an-

other person, he or she needed some kind of protection; for it was legal for a member of the slain person's family to try to avenge the blood of the slain relative. Genesis 9:6 established the principle of capital punishment, which was affirmed by Moses in Ex. 21:12–14. (Wiersbe, 61)

If the person was found to be innocent of premeditated murder, he or she was free to live in one of these cities until the high priest died. Then the person was allowed to go free anywhere in the territory of Israel.

At this point you may ask, "What does this have to do with whether a sinner can go to heaven or not?" Here are three truths that help us answer our question:

- **The cities of refuge were there to protect both parties.**

The avenger of blood would without doubt be very angry at the loss of his or her family member. The avenger would immediately want retribution and justice and needed to be protected from his or her emotion, to allow others to determine the justice of the matter (Deuteronomy 19:6, 12; Joshua 20:3–5). The innocent party also needed protection (Psalm 99:8).

- **The cities of refuge were God's plan to ensure proper judgment and justice.**

- **The cities of refuge were God's picture of His actions toward sinners for all time.**

The Bible teaches us of the universality of sin in every person's life (Romans 3:10–23). When we enter this life, we are unintentional sinners. As we live this life, we quickly become intentional sinners.

God the Father is the avenger of sin (1 Thessalonians 4:6). God the Son came as the redeemer (1 Timothy 2:4–5) to be the ransom for sinners (Mark 10:45). As God rescued Moses (Acts 7:10), He rescues all who call out to Him for salvation.

This is amazing to me this day. Jesus came to our home in this world. He came with a purpose (John 3:16). Every sinner who repents of his or her sin, and every sinner who asks for Jesus's forgiveness, and every sinner who surrenders his or her life to Jesus as Lord and Savior receives forgiveness of sin (1 John 1:7) and becomes heir of a home in heaven (Romans 8:17–18).

Right now I say to you—there is a place you can go. You can go to Jesus. You can also go to His true church. The church I pastor, First Baptist Church of Jackson, Georgia, is filled with people who were formerly broken, in-bondage sinners who blew it with God. You are welcome in our family because it is now your family because of Christ. Together we are looking for Jesus to come to take former sinners to the place called heaven.

I want to invite you to confess your sin and to repent of your sin. I invite you to say yes to Jesus as your Lord and Savior. Receive His forgiveness and receive His love into your life. I invite you into the family of His church. It is the best place to live as you wait for Jesus to come and take you to heaven!

ASSIGNMENTS FOR THE WEEK

DAY 1
Read 1 Samuel 21–25 and answer the following questions:

- What advice would you have given David as he fled to the Cave of Adullam?

- Why did David flee from the land of Israel? Why do we sometimes flee from the very God we so need?

DAY 2
Read 1 Samuel 26–30 and answer the following questions:

- What was in David's heart that kept him in a place where he spared Saul's life?

- How would you have felt if you had heard your enemy had been killed? Explain how God teaches us to react.

DAY 3
Read 2 Samuel 1–7 and answer the following questions:

- How does David's reaction to Saul's death mirror God's reaction when sinners die? Or does it?

- When David is anointed king in Israel, how does he live his life?

DAY 4

Read 2 Samuel 8–10 and answer the following questions:

- In chapter 9 David shows kindness. Explain what it means to receive the kindness of God.

- As long as we live here, there will be battles to fight. How does the truth of heaven help us to get through our battles?

DAY 5

Read 2 Samuel 11–7 and answer the following questions:

- David's sin is clear in chapter 11. Does his sin disqualify him from heaven? Explain and defend your answer.

- Did David give the same grace to his son whom God gave him? Explain.

CONCLUSION

It has been said that a successful journey begins with a first step. You and I have mentally made many steps in our studies together. There are some who have read this who began their journey in bondage and have been brought to a place of blessing by Jesus. Maybe you are still dealing with a reality without God. I want to share with you a story of a brother who was brought from a place of bondage into a place of blessing.

The brother's name is Jim (name changed). I met him one fall afternoon when I was a very young pastor. I can still see him sitting on his front porch in an old worn-out chair. Flying from his front porch was a Confederate flag. I had passed his house many times before. The person I was doing door-to-door visitation with had been very hesitant to stop. But on this fall afternoon I had convinced him to stop.

My partner parked our car on the street, and we got out. I greeted Jim with a hearty "Hello!" Jim never responded. We walked up to him and introduced ourselves. Jim lifted the beer he was holding and said, "Come on in. Can I offer you a beer?"

Very quickly it was easy to see that Jim had given in to the bondage he was in. He made no excuses, and he never offered to hide his bondage. I shared with him that we did not drink. He responded, "That's fine—that'll be more for me." Our visit was short. We never got beyond the porch. But God did something that day. God placed Jim on my heart. Over the next several months Jim and I became friends as I visited him weekly.

I did get beyond the porch. Jim shared with me that he was a veteran from the Vietnam War. It was in the war where the bondage began, and twenty-five years later it had taken its toll. Jim lived alone, with only so-called friends who came by to enjoy his beer. Each time I was with Jim I shared with him the blessed news of the gospel. I would tell him over and over about the God who came into our brokenness with the power to deliver us from our bondage. Each week I would ask Jim to give his life over to Jesus. Each week he would respond, "I can't do it, Pastor."

Months went by. I noticed that Jim seemed to be getting weaker and weaker. One week I went by and he was not home. A few days later I got a call from his mother. She said, "Jim is in the veterans' hospital with throat cancer. The doctors have operated and have given him a short time to live." The mother went on to tell me that he had not spoken since his surgery and asked if I would go by to see him. I assured her that I would go that day.

What happened next is Jim's story of trading his bondage for Jesus's blessing. The brother who had so many times visited Jim with me traveled with me to the hospital. We found Jim's room and were allowed to go in. As I walked into the ward, I saw that Jim's back was to the wall. I cried out to God, "Help me, Lord."

I spoke Jim's name, and he rolled over to look toward me. For the first time since I had known him, he smiled. I knew God was bringing him out of bondage. I asked Jim this question: "Jim, are you ready to surrender your life to Jesus?" He asked for the device that would help him communicate, raised it to his throat, and one word came out. It is a word that I will never forget. The word was "Yes."

For some this word may not seem to be significant, but to me it was. This word was both Jim's word of surrender and his word of victory. Jim would come out of the hospital and have the honor of living for one more year. In that year he told all of his former friends about the God who had brought him out of bondage and into a place of blessing.

As we end this book, I do not want you to end in bondage. Please say yes to Jesus today. Pray the following in true faith to Jesus:

- Jesus, I know You are God and I know You became a man to take my place on the cross (2 Corinthians 5:21).

- Jesus, I know You lived, died, were buried, and rose again on the third day (1 Corinthians 15:1–4).

- Jesus, forgive me of my sins. I repent of the wickedness of my rebellion (Luke 13:3).

- Jesus, come into my life and be my Lord and Savior (John 3:16).

- Jesus, I want to live for You (Mark 8:34–35).

- Jesus, I will tell my friends about You (1 Peter 3:15).

If you have prayed this prayer, we want to help you begin this journey of blessing. You can reach us at *www.jacksonfbc.com.*

Someday when the Lord comes to take me home to heaven, I will have completed my journey here, and I will experience the reality of heaven. I know I will see Jim there, and I look forward to seeing you there. This is the reality we need.

WORKS CITED

Duguid, Iain. *Numbers: God's Presence in the Wilderness.* Wheaton, Ill.: Crossway Publishing, 2006.

Gane, Roy. *The NIV Application Commentary: Leviticus, Numbers.* Grand Rapids: Zondervan Publishing, 2004.

Moody, Dwight L. *The Homework of Dwight L. Moody.* Albany, Oreg.: Books for the Ages, 1996.

Sprinkle, Joe M. *Leviticus and Numbers: Teach the Text Commentary Series.* Grand Rapids: Baker Books, 2015.

Sproul, R. C. *The Reformation Study Bible.* Lake Mary, Fla.: Ligonier Ministries, 2005.

Stubbs, David. *Numbers.* Grand Rapids: Brazos Press, 2009.

Wiersbe, Warren W. *The Wiersbe Bible Commentary: The Complete Old Testament in One Volume.* Colorado Springs: David C. Cook, 2007.